Judges

BOOKS IN THE "BIBLE STUDY COMMENTARY" SERIES

BIBLE STUDY COMMENTARY

Judges

PAUL P. ENNS

ZONDERVAN PUBLISHING HOUSE
OF THE ZONDERVAN CORPORATION
GRAND RAPIDS, MICHIGAN 49506

JUDGES: BIBLE STUDY COMMENTARY
Copyright © 1982 by The Zondervan Corporation
Grand Rapids, Michigan

Library of Congress Cataloging in Publication Data

Enns, Paul P., 1937–
    Judges, Bible study commentary.

    (Bible study commentary series)
    Bibliography: p.
    1. Bible. O.T. Judges—Commentaries. I. Title. II. Series.

BS1305.3.E5   222'.3207   82-2744
ISBN 0-310-44051-3   AACR2

Edited by John Danilson

Printed in the United States of America

84   85   86   87   88 — 10   9   8   7   6   5   4   3   2

To Terry,
beloved son, maturing in the faith

Contents

Introduction

A. Title of the Book

The title for the Book of Judges is taken from the Hebrew word *shephatim* ("judges"). The name relates to the leaders whom God raised up to deliver Israel from foreign oppression. The judges were usually called by God and served in military leadership as well as in religious and administrative functions.

The Book of Judges falls into the second category of the Hebrew canon called the Prophets and is listed among the former prophets, which includes Joshua, Judges, Samuel, and Kings.

B. Authorship

No clear statement or indication of authorship occurs in the book. The Talmud says Samuel was the author: "Samuel wrote the book which bears his name and the Book of Judges and Ruth" (Tractate Baba Bathra 14b). While tradition has merit, it cannot decisively confirm the authorship.

There is evidence that the book was completed early in Israel's monarchy. E. J. Young suggests that

> the book was compiled during the early days of the monarchy, either during the reign of Saul or the early days of David. It is quite possible that this author made use of sources, both oral and written, but the remarkable unity of the book's structure precludes any such scheme of compilation as that proposed by divisive criticism.[1]

---

[1]Edward J. Young, *An Introduction to the Old Testament* (Grand Rapids: Eerdmans, 1964), p. 170.

C. Date of Writing

Sufficient internal evidence points to a date early in Israel's monarchy: (1) the repetitious phrase "in those days Israel had no king; everyone did as he saw fit" suggests a date following the establishment of the monarchy under Saul (cf. 17:6; 18:1; 19:1; 21:25);[2] (2) the statement of 1:21 that "to this day the Jebusites live there with the Benjamites" indicates the book was completed prior to David's conquest of Jerusalem (2 Sam. 5:6–7); (3) Judges 1:29 indicates the Canaanites persisted in living in Gezer, suggesting the book was written prior to 970 B.C. when the Egyptians captured Gezer and gave the city to Solomon as a wedding present for his daughter (1 Kings 9:16); (4) Sidon, rather than Tyre, is mentioned as the chief Phoenician city, affirming a date prior to the twelfth century B.C. when Tyre emerged as the greater of the two (3:3).

D. Date of the Events

There are two divergent views concerning the length of the period of the judges. Proponents of both views agree the period began with the death of Joshua and ended with the institution of the monarchy under Saul (about 1043 B.C.). Most liberal writers and some conservatives hold to the late date for the Exodus, thereby limiting the period of the judges to only 150 or 180 years.[3] The major problem with this view is that insufficient time is allowed for the periods of office, even while recognizing that the terms of some judges overlapped. Moreover, the intrinsic evidence (11:26) demands a period longer than 150 or 180 years.[4] Many conservative writers hold to an early date for the Exodus (1446 B.C.) and therefore suggest a period of nearly 350 years (*about* 1390–1043 B.C.).[5]

---

[2]Unless otherwise indicated (e.g. by context), references refer to the Book of Judges when the Bible book is not given. Direct Bible quotations are from the New International Version unless specified otherwise.

[3]For example, John Bright suggests the period of the judges lasted from 1200–1050 B.C. (cf. John Bright, *A History of Israel*, 2nd ed. [Philadelphia: Westminster, 1972], p. 166). Cundall suggests a period from 1200–1020 B.C. (cf. Arthur E. Cundall and Leon Morris, *Judges and Ruth* [Chicago: Inter-Varsity Press, 1968], p. 30).

[4]For a detailed discussion of the early date of the Exodus that allows sufficient time chronologically for all the judges, see Leon Wood, *A Survey of Israel's History* [Grand Rapids: Zondervan, 1970], pp. 88–109. The argument rests on the literal use of the numbers recorded in 1 Kings 6:1 and Judges 11:26.

[5]John Davis suggests a period of 337 years (1380–1043 B.C.) (cf. John J. Davis, *Conquest and Crisis: Studies in Joshua, Judges and Ruth* [Grand Rapids: Baker, 1969], p. 94). Leon Wood advocates a period of 340 years (1390–1050 B.C.) (cf. Leon Wood, *Distressing Days of the Judges* [Grand Rapids: Zondervan, 1975], p. 11).

E. Function of the Judges

The basic meaning of the Hebrew verb form *shaphat* is *"act as law-giver, judge, governor* (giving law, deciding controversies and executing law, civil, religious, political, social; both early and late)."[6] It is so used in 2:16–19; 3:10; 4:4; 10:2–3; 11:27. F. F. Bruce cites related usages of the term:

> The word *sepetim* is cognate with the Phoenician word by which, according to Roman writers, the chief magistrates of Carthage were known 1,000 years later (suffetes). In the Samaritan records the judges are called 'kings.'[7]

While the basic concept of the judge is understood in the judicial sense of administering justice, the term also denotes leadership and administration. Leon Wood explains:

> The unique meaning does not exclude the more common one, but adds to it a basic and more inclusive concept. Put briefly, that concept is "service as leader." The judges of the period in view, then, were persons who "served as leaders" of the people. This leadership need not have excluded the work of deciding cases, especially when major problems were involved, but it centered in the disposal of administrative duties necessary to leadership.[8]

In addition the judges also served in a military capacity as is clearly seen in the cases of Othniel, Ehud, Deborah, Gideon, Jephthah, and Samson. A major function of each judge was to deliver a region or district of Israel from enslavement by an oppressor after the people had learned the lesson of God's chastisement.

Finally, the judges were understood to be "special agents of divine power,"[9] functioning in a true sense in a mediatorial role. They were recognized as having been raised up by God to deliver the people and therefore were understood to have special divine favor resting on them.

F. Theme of the Book of Judges

In contrast to the theme of victory found in the Book of Joshua, the major subject of Judges concerns the apostasy, failure, and defeat of the

---

[6]Francis Brown, S. R. Driver, and Charles A. Briggs, *A Hebrew and English Lexicon of the Old Testament* (Oxford: At the Clarendon Press, 1968), p. 1047.

[7]F. F. Bruce, "Judges," *New Bible Commentary: Revised*, (Grand Rapids: Eerdmans, 1970), p. 252.

[8]Wood, *Distressing Days*, p. 4.

[9]William Foxwell Albright, *From the Stone Age to Christianity* (Garden City, N.Y.: Doubleday, 1957), p. 284.

Israelites. All the successes enjoyed by the nation under Joshua stand in contrast to the periods of oppression by their enemies during the time of the Book of Judges. The reason for Israel's failure and defeat in Judges was national disunity and disobedience.

The key to the chaotic conditions is found in the recurring phrase "in those days Israel had no king; everyone did as he saw fit" (cf. 17:6; 18:1; 19:1; 21:25). During the time of the judges Israel had no leaders of the stature of Moses or Joshua who could turn the people back to the observance of God's law.

G. Purpose of the Book of Judges

Immediately prior to Israel's entrance into the land under Joshua, God promised great blessings for the nation (Deut. 11:18–25). Conditioned on their obedience to the Mosaic covenant enacted at Sinai (Exod. 19–40), God promised Israel victory over the inhabitants of the land, appropriation of a vast territory, and a continuing conquest of their enemies. A primary purpose of the writer of the Book of Judges was to explain why Israel failed to experience the blessings of God.[10] Israel sinned in disobeying God and thereby forfeited God's blessings during that period.

The chaotic state precipitated by Israel's disobedience brought about the need for a singular, authoritative leadership later reflected in the monarchy. Thus a further purpose of the Book of Judges "was to show that a centralized hereditary kingship was necessary for the well-being of the Covenant theocracy."[11] Israel's history in the period of the united monarchy, and particularly in the reign of David, indicated the need for a centralized monarchy that would unite the nation. The Book of Judges thus forms a transitional bridge from the divinely appointed leaders, Moses and Joshua, to the beginning of the monarchy under Saul.

H. Historical Setting

Much work remained to be done although Joshua had led the Israelites to tremendous and important victories in three major campaigns. The land had not been fully possessed and groups of heathen tribes were still entrenched. At the conclusion of Joshua's life large areas of land still remained to be conquered (Josh. 13:1).

---

[10]Wood, *Distressing Days*, p. 135.
[11]R. K. Harrison, *Introduction to the Old Testament* (Grand Rapids: Eerdmans, 1969), p. 692.

The Book of Judges thus deals with the period following the initial conquest of Israel, covering over three hundred years—from approximately 1390 B.C. until the rise of Saul in 1043 B.C. The period of the judges coincides with the conclusion of the Late Bronze Age and the beginning of the Iron Age (about 1200 B.C.). The Canaanites apparently had a monopoly on iron, which proved a major problem for Israel. Although Judah "took possession of the hill country . . . they were unable to drive the people from the plains, because they had iron chariots" (1:19). One of the oppressors of Israel was Jabin, who marshaled an army under Sisera and overpowered Israel with chariots (4:3, 13). The Philistines retained a monopoly on iron until the days of Saul (1 Sam. 13:19–22).

I. Outline of the Book

The Book of Judges can be divided into three major parts. Part One: The Causes for the Period of the Judges (1:1–3:6) describes the disobedience, idolatry, and intermarriage of the Israelites in bringing about the chaotic conditions of the period; Part Two: The Conditions During the Period of the Judges (3:7–16:31), narrates the cycles of sin, oppression, and deliverance; and Part Three: The Consequences of the Period of the Judges (17:1–21:25) describes the resultant chaos during the time of the judges.

Part One: Causes for the Period of the Judges (1:1–3:6)
    Chapter 1: Incomplete Obedience (1:1–2:5)
        A. Israel's disobedience (1:1–36)
           1. Incomplete victory of Judah (1:1–20)
           2. Incomplete victory of Benjamin (1:21)
           3. Incomplete victory of Manasseh (1:22–28)
           4. Incomplete victory of Ephraim (1:29)
           5. Incomplete victory of Zebulun (1:30)
           6. Incomplete victory of Asher (1:31–32)
           7. Incomplete victory of Naphtali (1:33)
           8. Incomplete victory of Dan (1:34–36)
        B. God's disapproval (2:1–5)
           1. Reiteration of God's covenant (2:1)
           2. Affliction of Israel (2:2–3)
           3. Dejection of Israel (2:4–5)

PART ONE:

CAUSES FOR THE PERIOD
OF THE JUDGES

Chapter 1

Incomplete Obedience
(Judges 1:1–2:5)

The opening chapters of Judges are important in that they explain the causes of the chaotic conditions of the period that the book covers. Israel failed to fully appropriate the blessings of the land because they did not completely drive out the enemy. The detailed account of 1:1–36 emphasizes this disobedience. The conditions of this period are further explained by Israel's transgression into idolatry and intermarriage with the Canaanites.

The continuity of Joshua and Judges is seen in the repetitive accounts in the opening chapters of Judges:

Event	Joshua	Judges
Benjamin unable to conquer Jerusalem	15:63	1:21
Caleb gives daughter to Othniel	15:15–19	1:11–15
Caleb drives out the three sons of Anak	15:14	1:20
Manasseh is unable to conquer Canaanites	17:11–13	1:27–28
Ephraim is unable to drive out Canaanites	16:10	1:29
Death of Joshua	24:28–31	2:6–10

A. Israel's disobedience (1:1–36)

1. *Incomplete victory of Judah* (1:1–20)

Shortly before dying, the aged warrior Joshua summoned the Israelites and reminded them of the necessity of completing the conquest of the land (Josh. 24:1–27). The Book of Judges opens with Israel responding to Joshua's injunction by looking to the Lord for guidance. Thus after Joshua's death the Israelites asked, "Who will be the first to go up and fight for us against the Canaanites?" (1:1). The term Canaanite may be used in a broad or narrower sense; in the broad sense it is a general designation for the enemies of Israel inhabiting the Promised Land. Genesis 10:15–19 indicates Canaan was the father of many people, among them the Jebusites, Amorites, Girgashites, and Hivites. The Canaanites worshiped Baal, a male fertility god, and his female consort, Asherah (variously termed Astarte or Ashtaroth). Since they believed the sexual union of Baal and Asherah produced their crops, the worship of the Canaanites consisted of temple prostitution to enhance the productivity of their crops.[1]

The indication is that the Israelites inquired of the Lord through the Urim and Thummim (Num. 27:21). In response to the question of which tribe should be the first to go to war against the Canaanites, the Lord designated Judah. Since Judah was the largest tribe as well as the kingly tribe, it was logical that Judah should be the first to go up to battle. In the Lord's response there was also the promise of success: "I have given the land into their hands" (1:2).[2]

In response to the Lord's promise, the men of Judah summoned their brothers, the Simeonites, to join them in battle against the Canaanites (1:3). The alliance of these two tribes was natural. One reason was that Judah and Simeon were both children of Leah (Gen. 29:33, 35); furthermore, the territory allotted to Simeon was limited to cities within the territory of Judah (Josh. 19:1–9).

The assistance was to be mutual: the Simeonites would assist the Judahites in exterminating the Canaanites from their territory. Later the men of Judah would help the Simeonites. As the two tribes joined forces, the Lord gave them victory over the Canaanites and Perizzites, and they struck down ten thousand men at Bezek (1:4). The Perizzites were in the land prior to the time of Abraham (cf. Gen. 15:20) and are generally thought to have been hill-dwellers, their name designating them as villagers rather than an ethnic group.[3] It is possible the terms Canaanites and Perizzites are general names that denote the two major

---

[1]See Roland de Vaux, *Ancient Israel* (New York: McGraw-Hill, 1965), pp. 284–288. For a helpful discussion regarding the moral problem in the command to exterminate the Canaanites, see Merrill F. Unger, *Archaeology and the Old Testament* (Grand Rapids: Zondervan, 1954), pp. 175–77.

[2]The emphatic Hebrew term *hinay* ("Behold!") "introduces a clause involving predication," Brown, Driver, and Briggs, *Hebrew and English Lexicon* (Oxford: At the Clarendon Press, 1968), p. 244. The statement emphasizes success—conditioned, of course, on Israel's obedience.

[3]J. D. Douglas, ed., *The New Bible Dictionary*, NBD (Grand Rapids: Eerdmans, 1962), p. 968.

groups in the land; thus the Canaanites may refer to the inhabitants along the coast and the Perizzites to the dwellers of the central hill country. In this sense the two terms may be similar to the general designations Canaanite and Amorite (cf. Josh. 5:1).

The Israelites defeated the enemy at Bezek. Some suggest Bezek lay near Jerusalem, but more likely it was situated near Mount Gilboa, southeast of Jezreel and southwest of the Sea of Galilee.[4]

A general statement of the conquest is given in 1:4, while a specific account of the defeat and capture of the king is given in verses 5–7. The designation "Adoni-Bezek" ("Lord of Bezek") is a title rather than a proper name. In the pursuit Adoni-Bezek was seized; his captors then cut off his thumbs and big toes (v. 6). The barbarous action was the law of *lex talionis*—"an eye for an eye and a tooth for a tooth." The mutilation rendered the individual unfit for military service, since he could no longer use a sword or run in battle. The justification for the action in the prevailing culture is seen in the resignation of the king; he recognized that what he had done to others now had been inflicted on him (1:7).

While some commentators suggest that Adoni-Bezek's reference to seventy kings is hyperbolic, it is possible the seventy were "conquered by him at successive times, and some of them were successive chieftains over the same towns or clans."[5] The phrase "picked up scraps under my table" indicates the defeated kings were treated like dogs by Adoni-Bezek (cf. Matt. 15:27). Adoni-Bezek was brought to Jerusalem where he died (1:7).

The king of Jerusalem had been killed during Joshua's campaign (cf. Josh. 10:22–27; 12:10), but the city had not been captured at that time. Although Jerusalem was now in the hands of the men of Judah (1:8), not all the Jebusites were expelled (cf. Josh. 15:63; Judg. 1:21). It appears the Israelites lost the city soon after its capture and did not regain permanent possession of it until the time of David (2 Sam. 5:6–7).

Jerusalem is one of the oldest occupied cities in the world, having been inhabited for five thousand years. The earliest Scripture reference to Jerusalem speaks of "Melchizedek king of Salem" (Gen. 14:18).

---

[4]Walter C. Kaiser, Jr., "Bezek," *The Zondervan Pictorial Encyclopedia of the Bible* (ZPEB), Merrill C. Tenney, gen. ed. (Grand Rapids: Zondervan, 1975), 1:554; Yohanan Aharoni and Michael Avi-Yonah, *The Macmillan Bible Atlas* (New York: Macmillan, 1968), p. 60.

[5]A. R. Fausset, *A Critical and Expository Commentary on the Book of Judges* (Minneapolis: James & Klock Publishing Co., 1977 reprint), p. 13.

The city is identified as Urushalim in the Egyptian execration texts of the nineteenth century B.C.

The statement in 1:9 provides a summary of Judah's conquest in the land. The three terms "the hill country, the Negev and the western foothills" denote the three geographical areas of the southern portion of the land. The hill country specifies the central mountainous area that includes the cities of Jerusalem and Hebron and rises to more than three thousand feet above sea level. The Negev refers to the arid territory south of Hebron and includes the cities of Beersheba and Kadesh Barnea. The western foothills, also called the Shephelah, indicates the territory between the coastal plain and the central mountain ridge.

The men of Judah then carried their battle south to Hebron, a city situated about twenty miles south of Jerusalem, and lying twenty-eight hundred feet above sea level in a valley between two mountain ridges. Hebron was formerly known as Kiriath Arba ("city of four") which name indicates it was a tetrapolis. Arba, the greatest man of the Anakites, may have founded the city (Josh. 14:15). Hebron was also of significance to Israel since Abraham had lived there (Gen. 13:18).

The faith of the men of Judah is seen in the conquest inasmuch as the three individuals mentioned (1:10) were sons of Anak and were notorious for their stature and valor in battle (1:20).

Following the conquest of Hebron, the Judahites attacked Debir, a city about thirteen miles southwest of Hebron. No adequate explanation for the name Kiriath Sepher ("city of books") has been discovered (1:11).

Debir must have been formidable since Caleb promised the conqueror of the city his daughter Acsah for his wife (1:12). Caleb's younger brother, Othniel (cf. Josh. 15:17; Judg. 1:13; 3:9), conquered Debir and married Acsah (1:13). Othniel later became the first judge of Israel.

Since Acsah had previously received land in the Negev from her father, she came to him requesting the springs of water, an essential in the southern arid land (1:15). Caleb acceded to her wish and gave her the upper and lower springs. The springs can be identified with cisterns or reservoirs in Sel ed-Dilbe, southwest of Hebron, or shafts that provide access to ground water at Tell Beit Mirsim.[6]

[6]See H. G. May, "Joshua," *Peake's Commentary on the Bible* (New York: Thomas Nelson and Sons Ltd., 1962), p. 299; Charles F. Pfeiffer, "Judges," *The Wycliffe Bible Commentary*, WBC (Chicago: Moody Press, 1962), p. 235.

The Kenites are mentioned (1:16) because they joined Israel in the quest for the Promised Land (Num. 10:29–34). Moses was associated with the Kenites through his marriage to Zipporah, the daughter of Jethro (Exod. 2:16–22). The term "father-in-law" can also be read "brother-in-law" since the Hebrew consonants are exactly the same for both. The Hebrew word literally means "circumciser, hence father-in-law, with ref. to circumcision performed on young men just before marriage."[7] The word should be understood as father-in-law in both 1:16 and 4:11.

The Kenites, whose name means metalworkers, were a nomadic people who now entered the land with the Israelites. The designation "City of Palms" is normally understood to refer to Jericho. Some suggest in this instance it cannot refer to Jericho because of the context;[8] however, the movement of the Kenites in 1:16 indicates Jericho is meant. The text suggests the Kenites joined the Israelites in entering the land at Jericho. Following Israel's movement southward, the Kenites also moved south to live in the Desert of Judah in the Negev near Arad. Tell Arad is located about twenty-two and a half miles east-northeast of Beersheba. Nelson Glueck describes the strategic location as seen today:

> A good agricultural area, dry-farmed today with the frequent result of bumper crops, contributed to its growth and prominence. Anchored securely on a rise in the center of a wide, slightly rolling plain, its robust mound has withstood the violence of the elements and the vandalism of man.... The knoll on which it stands is the apex of a gently sloping watershed, which separates two groups of wadis of unequal size. A short distance to the east of it commence the outrunners of several of them, that increase speedily in size and depth. Reinforced with growing branches, they soon rip their way down abrupt terraces and steep hillsides to empty at separate places into the dead-end trough of the Sea of Salt.[9]

In order to avenge a previous defeat, the men of Judah joined the Simeonites in a battle against the city of Zephath which had been allotted to Simeon (Josh. 19:4). The city is known to have been in the general area of Beersheba, but a more precise identification has not been made positively.

Following their failure at Kadesh Barnea, the Israelites tried to in-

---

[7]Brown, Driver, and Briggs, *Hebrew and English Lexicon*, p. 368.
[8]Bruce, "Judges," NBC, p. 257; Cundall and Morris, *Judges and Ruth* p. 56.
[9]Nelson Glueck, *Rivers in the Desert* (New York: W. W. Norton & Co., 1968), pp. 51–52.

vade the land without the Lord's sanction. The result was devastating: the Amalekites and Canaanites pursued the fleeing Israelites and beat them down all the way to Hormah (Num. 14:45). The city had been conquered earlier (Num. 21:2–3) but apparently had been reoccupied by the Canaanites. At that time Israel had vowed to give the city up to entire destruction; and that was now carried out. The Israelites totally destroyed the city of Zephath (1:17), at which time they called the city Hormah derived its name from a common root word *herem*, which means "devoting to destruction cities of Canaanites and other neighbours of Isr., *exterminating* inhabitants, and destroying or appropriating their possessions."[10] The city that had been devoted to pagan worship and opposition to Israel was now devoted to God for destruction.

The men of Judah turned westward toward the coastal plain. In the appropriation of their territory, they captured the three principal cities of the Philistines, Gaza, Ashkelon, and Ekron (1:18). The invasion took place from the south as Israel first captured Gaza, the most southerly city, and then moved northward to successively take Ashkelon and Ekron.

The summary statement recorded in 1:19 indicates the Lord provided the victory for the tribe of Judah, enabling it to capture the hill country. The men of Judah, however, were unable to drive the Canaanites from the plains because the enemy had iron chariots. The Canaanites had learned the secret of iron from the Hittites and now maintained a monopoly on iron (cf. 1 Sam. 13:19–22). While the Canaanites with their iron chariots were formidable opponents, God had nonetheless promised victory to Israel (Deut. 20:3–4). The failure must be understood as a lack of faith on the part of Israel.[11] Israel's great victory over Jabin with his many chariots at Hazor should not have been forgotten (Josh. 11).

The statement in 1:20 follows logically. Following Judah's conquest of the hill country, Caleb was given Hebron as he had been promised. The accounts of Caleb's conquest and his defeat of the three sons of Anak are also mentioned in Joshua (15:13–14).

---

[10]Brown, Driver, and Briggs, *Hebrew and English Lexicon*, p. 355. For additional study see the author's work, *Joshua: A Bible Study Commentary* (Grand Rapids: Zondervan, 1981), pp. 79–80.

[11]Paulus Cassel, "The Book of Judges" in *Lange's Commentary on the Holy Scriptures* (Grand Rapids: Zondervan, 1960 reprint), p. 39.

2. *Incomplete victory of Benjamin* (1:21)

The ensuing verses further introduce the reader to the imcomplete obedience of the Israelites. They failed to drive out the inhabitants of the land, establishing a situation that would result in idolatry, inter-marriage, and, as a result, corruption of the nation.

The Jebusites remained entrenched in Jerusalem, and they possessed the city until it was captured by David in 1003 B.C. (2 Sam. 5:6–7).

3. *Incomplete victory of Manasseh* (1:22–28)

The house of Joseph, which refers to Ephraim and Manasseh, fol-lowed the leadership of Judah and also attacked their enemies, the inhabitants of Bethel (1:22). Although Bethel had been allied with Ai against Israel (Josh. 8), there is no mention of the conquest of Bethel at that time. The city lay on the border of Benjamin and Ephraim. Al-though Bethel was allotted to Benjamin, Ephraim attacked the city because of Bethel's intrusion into Ephraimite territory.

The Israelites sent spies to Bethel, and they received information from a man coming out of the city (1:24). Why did they need to get information about the entrance of the city? No doubt these Israelites going up to battle against Bethel had not been part of the small group that originally went up to Ai to fight; hence, they needed to gain knowledge of the city.

Having secured the necessary information, the Israelites "put the city to the sword but spared the man and his whole family" (1:25). The extermination of the city was in accord with the command of God (Deut. 20:16–17); it was necessary in order to prevent the corruption of Israel by the immoral practices of the Canaanites (Deut. 7:1–5). The conquest of Bethel was important for Israel since God had revealed Himself there to the patriarch Jacob whereupon he changed its name from Luz to Bethel, meaning "house of God" (Gen. 28:10–19).

The man who had provided the information left the area, going up to the land of the Hittites, perhaps northern Syria. The great Hittite Empire existed from about 1900–1200 B.C. and encompassed a large area from Asia Minor to the Euphrates River. Until Hugo Winckler of Berlin discovered about ten thousand clay tablets at Boghazkoy in 1906, nothing was known about the Hittites apart from what was re-corded in Scripture.[12]

---

[12]R. K. Harrison, *Old Testament Times* (Grand Rapids: Eerdmans, 1970), pp. 89–92.

Manasseh's failure to capture the cities mantioned in 1:27 is significant since these cities occupied strategic locations in the valleys of Jezreel and Esdraelon. These Canaanite city-states commanded the passes through the hills to the great central plain and were located on the major trade routes from south to north. The Canaanite occupation of these cities divided the nation of Israel physically, while the Canaanites remained entrenched in the valleys where they were able to utilize their chariots.[13]

Beth Shan lay at the eastern end of Manasseh's territory where the Valley of Jezreel joins the Jordan Valley. Taanach was located along the Via Maris where the important route enters the hill country from the Plain of Sharon. The city of Dor lay on the Mediterranean coast just south of Mount Carmel. These three cities spanned the northern boundary of Manasseh's territory. Ibleam, located in the north central territory of Manasseh, was significant because it guarded the route to Dothan and the coastal plain. Megiddo, along with Taanach, guarded the main pass on the Via Maris leading from the Jezreel Valley to the Plain of Sharon.

Although the Israelites did not totally expel the Canaanites, "they pressed the Canaanites into forced labor" (1:28). The term "forced labor" denotes slave-gangs, and the same term was used to describe Israel's bondage to their oppressors in Egypt (Exod. 1:11).[14]

4. Incomplete victory of Ephraim (1:29)

The failure of Ephraim to drive the Canaanites out of Gezer was a further indication that the integration of Israel and the Canaanites was beginning to permeate the entire land. The city of Gezer was eighteen miles northwest of Jerusalem, near the border of the Shephelah and the coastal plain. Gezer was ultimately conquered by Pharaoh and given to Solomon (1 Kings 9:16), indicating Judges was written prior to the time of Solomon.

5. Incomplete victory of Zebulun (1:30)

Israel's failure to drive out the Canaanites now spread northward as Zebulun failed to rid their territory of their enemy. Neither Kitron nor Nahalol has been identified with certainty.

---

[13]Cundall and Morris, *Judges and Ruth*, p. 59; John Gray, "Joshua, Judges and Ruth" in The Century Bible, CB (Greenwood, S.C.: The Attic Press, 1967), p. 157.

[14]Brown, Driver, and Briggs, *Hebrew and English Lexicon*, p. 587.

6. *Incomplete victory of Asher* (1:31–32)

The northern tribe of Asher also failed to drive out the Canaanites who remained entrenched in their cities. The problem intensified for the Israelites as the Canaanite resistance increased. There is a significant change in phraseology in 1:32. Previously the narrator stated that the Canaanites continued to live among the Israelites (cf. 1:27, 29, 30); now, however, the text states that "the people of Asher lived among the Canaanite inhabitants," indicating stronger resistance. The people of Asher failed to capture seven of the twenty-two cities allotted to them (Josh. 19:30). Acco (modern Acre), Sidon, and Aczib were important coastal cities north of Mount Carmel. Sidon was the oldest Phoenician city, being mentioned as early as Genesis 10:19. The Canaanites of this area maintained their strength and developed the maritime kingdom of Phoenicia, with which David and Solomon entered into an alliance (2 Sam. 5:11; 1 Kings 5:1–12).[15] A resultant tragedy was Ahab's marriage to Jezebel, a Sidonian, who introduced Baal worship into Israel (1 Kings 16:31).

7. *Incomplete victory of Naphtali* (1:33)

The breakdown of Israel's dominance over the Canaanites is further seen in the strong resistance in the territory of Naphtali. This is again evidenced in the statement that "the Naphtalites too lived among the Canaanite inhabitants of the land."

The locations of the two Canaanite strongholds, Beth Shemesh and Beth Anath, have not been positively indentified. Aharoni suggests the northern part of Upper Galilee as a probability.[16] The names of the cities, however, are significant. Beth Shemesh means "house of the sun," while Beth Anath means "house of Anath." Both of these were Canaanite shrines, the former being a shrine to Shemesh, the sun-god, while the latter honored Anath, the fertility goddess and consort of Baal. The emphasis is clear that idolatry remained entrenched in the land and was a problem that would ultimately destroy the moral fiber of the nation.

8. *Incomplete victory of Dan* (1:34–36)

The term Amorites is used synonymously with Canaanites and normally designates those occupying the central hill country. The oppo-

---

[15]Cundall and Morris, *Judges and Ruth*, p. 61.

[16]Yohanan Aharoni, *The Land of the Bible* (Philadelphia: Westminster, 1967), p. 214.

sition to the Israelites intensified as the Amorites restricted the Danites to the hill country, not permitting them to occupy the cities they had inherited in the plain (cf. Josh. 19:41–46). Eventually, the Danites moved to the extreme north (18:1–31).

The Amorite persistence in maintaining the three cities of 1:35 was significant, for these cities "probably dominated the main route from Jerusalem and the central highlands to the coastal plain, thus driving another lesser wedge into Israelite territory."[17] Mount Heres ("sun mountain") was located fifteen miles northwest of Jerusalem and possibly was the site of southern Beth Shemesh; Aijalon lay in the valley eleven miles northwest of Jerusalem, while Shaalbim was northwest of Aijalon. The extent of Amorite dominance is seen in the statement in 1:36. The Amorites controlled a territory that extended south and east to the important Scorpion Pass, which ascended from the southwest corner of the Dead Sea toward Beersheba and formed the northern border of the Desert of Zin.

Although the Danites were unable to subjugate the Amorites, the house of Joseph—Ephraim and Manasseh, the northern neighbors of Dan—eventually reduced the Amorites to forced labor (1:35).

Several things evidenced Israel's weakened and problematic condition: (1) The Canaanites remained entrenched in the land since Israel was unable to drive them out. (2) Because of Canaanite strongholds throughout the land, Israel was unable to move about freely. (3) Canaanite idolatry remained intact in the land—a problem that would ultimately lead Israel into apostasy. (4) Instead of rejecting and removing the Canaanites from the land, Israel developed a relationship with them.

B. God's disapproval (2:1–5)

1. Reiteration of God's covenant (2:1)

As a result of Israel's disobedience and failure, the angel of the Lord came to announce a message of judgment. The angel of the Lord is a theophany, a visible manifestation of God. The same One appeared to Joshua (Josh. 5:13–15) and later appeared to Gideon (6:11–24) and the family of Danites (13:3–23). The Jewish Targums and the rabbis thought the angel of the Lord was an earthly messenger, either Phinehas or Joshua, but no prophet ever identified himself so com-

---

[17]Cundall and Morris, *Judges and Ruth*, p. 62.

pletely with the Lord. "The prophets always distinquish between themselves and Jehovah, by introducing their words with the declaration 'thus saith Jehovah.'"[18]

The angel of the Lord came up from Gilgal, the place where Israel had placed the memorial stones and rested after crossing the Jordan. It was here that the angel of the Lord had earlier appeared to Joshua to announce the conquest of Jericho (Josh. 5:13–15). Now, however, the announcement concerned chastisement. The designation Gilgal appears to indicate the message came from the presence of the Lord since Gilgal was the initial resting place of the ark (although later is was moved to Shiloh, Josh. 18:1). The site of Bokim is uncertain; possibly it was between Gilgal and Shiloh.

The angel reminded the Israelites of the Lord's faithfulness in bringing them out of Egypt and into the land He had promised them (cf. Gen. 12:1–3; 15:12–21; 17:7–8; Josh. 1:6).

2. *Affliction of Israel* (2:2–3)

In his rebuke the angel of the Lord reminded the Israelites of the Lord's previous commands, saying, "And you shall not make a covenant with the people of this land, but you shall break down their altars" (2:2; cf. Exod. 23:32; 34:13). Israel had broken her covenant with the Lord. They had failed in two areas: they had made a covenant with the inhabitants (with the Gibeonites, Josh. 9:1–27; and with the Canaanites in permitting them to live or serve in forced labor, 1:28, 30, 33), and they had failed to tear down the altars of idolatry.

As a result the Lord warned that He would not drive out the Canaanites; instead, they would become as thorns in the sides of the Israelites (2:3). It is possible the word translated "snare" is related to the Assyrian *saddu*

> meaning "net", "snare" or "trap" and makes the whole section a sustained metaphor, in other words the inhabitants will be traps into which the Israelites will stumble by being led astray to worship the gods of the country, and the gods will be the striker which pins them down so that they cannot escape. Here the reference is to a type of bird snare still familiar in Palestine in which the victim, flying into a trap, actuates a spring which causes it to be knocked down or pierced.[19]

---

[18]C. F. Keil and F. Delitzsch, *Joshua, Judges, Ruth* in *Biblical Commentary on the Old Testament* (Grand Rapids: Eerdmans, 1968 reprint), p. 264.
[19]Cundall and Morris, *Judges and Ruth*, pp. 65–66.

3. *Dejection of Israel* (2:4–5)

On hearing the pronouncement of the judgment, the Israelites wept: as a result the name of that place was called Bokim ("weepers"). The sorrow of the Israelites is further observed in their offering of sacrifices (cf. Lev. 1–7). Some commentators suggest the ritual took place at the tabernacle; however, Keil and Delitzsch suggest sacrifices were offered in any place where the Lord appeared to the people (cf. Deut. 12:5; Judg. 6:20, 26, 28; 13:16; 2 Sam. 24:25).[20]

For Further Study

1. Read an article on Judges in a Bible dictionary or encyclopedia.

2. Analyze the failures in chapter 1 in the light of God's promise (Deut. 11:22–25; Josh. 1:1–8).

3. What important principles concerning success and failure can be gleaned from chapter 1?

---

[20]Keil and Delitzsch, *Joshua, Judges, Ruth*, p. 266.

Chapter 2

Idolatry and Intermarriage
(Judges 2:6–3:6)

The further degeneration of Israel is seen in their reversion to idolatry following the death of Joshua. Having forsaken the Lord, the generation following Joshua turned to the religion of the Canaanites. The apostasy was intensified through intermarriage with pagans, assuring Israel's bondage to their polytheistic neighbors. As a result the sinning cycles of the apostate nation began; the holiness of a righteous God demanded the punishment of the disobedient nation, yet the mercy of God was manifest when the nation turned in repentance.

A. Transition from Joshua (2:6–9)

This section is similar to Joshua 24:29–31 in describing the death and burial of Joshua and serves as a connecting link between the narrative of Joshua and Judges. Joshua dismissed the Israelites from Shechem where he had gathered them to rehearse their obligations to the Lord under the suzerainty-vassal treaty (Josh. 24:1–28). The Israelites returned to their own allotted territories to eliminate the last vestiges of Canaanite presence (2:6). The people served the Lord throughout the lifetime of Joshua and the elders who outlived him and who had seen the great works of the Lord (2:7). The account of Judges intensifies the knowledge and responsibility of the Israelites, for where Joshua emphasizes that the elders "experienced everything the Lord had done for Israel" (Josh. 24:31), Judges emphasizes that the elders "had *seen* all the *great* things the Lord had done for Israel" (2:7). Joshua's generation had witnessed the great acts of God delivering Israel from Egypt—the Exodus and the provisions in the desert; they had seen the great power of God manifested in crossing the Jordan River and con-

quering the city-states in the land. Joshua and the elders of his generation influenced the people in obeying the Lord, but upon their death
the nation departed in their loyalty to God.

In describing the death of Joshua, the narrator designates the aged
warrior as "the servant of the LORD" (2:8), a phrase previously used to
describe Moses (Josh. 1:1), but also a title used to describe kings
(2 Sam. 3:18; 2 Chron. 32:16), and ultimately Messiah (Isa. 52:13;
53:11). When Moses died Joshua was appointed his successor (Josh.
1:1–9); but at the death of Joshua no mention is made of a successor,
perhaps in anticipation of the chaotic period of the judges.

Joshua died at the age of a hundred and ten and was buried at
Timnath Heres (also known as Timnath Serah, cf. Josh. 19:50; 24:30) in
the hill country of Ephraim (2:9). Samaritan tradition identifies Timnath Heres with Kafr-Haris, ten miles southwest of Shechem; however, there is no archaeological support for the site. Timnath Heres,
which means portion of the sun, may actually be Khirbet Tibneh,
seventeen miles from Jerusalem and Shechem.

B. Transgression of Israel (2:10)

The phrase "gathered to their fathers" is synonymous with "gathered
to his people" (cf. Gen. 25:8, 17; 35:29) and

> denotes the reunion in Sheol with friends who have gone before, and
> therefore presupposes faith in the personal continuance of a man after
> death, as a presentiment which the promises of God had exalted in the
> case of the patriarchs into a firm assurance of faith (Heb. xi. 13).[1]

The generation that grew up following the death of Joshua and his
generation were unfamiliar with the Lord and His works. The expression "who knew neither the Lord" is explained in the following phrase
"nor what he had done for Israel." The new generation had not witnessed the great deeds of the Lord on behalf of Israel as the nation
entered the land. The lack of acquaintance with the Lord's works also
suggests the failure of the previous generation to communicate the
truth concerning God to the succeeding generation (cf. Deut. 6:7). The

---

[1]C. F. Keil and F. Delitzsch, *The Pentateuch* in *Biblical Commentary on the Old
Testament*, 3 vols. 1:263; G. A. Cooke suggests the expression originally referred to the
family sepulcher, then to the shadowy life of Sheol, and finally as a euphemism for death;
cf. G. A. Cooke, "The Book of Judges" in *The Cambridge Bible for Schools and Colleges*
(Cambridge: at the University Press, 1913), p. 28. Boling rejects the suggestion that it is
a euphemism for death; cf. Robert G. Boling, "Judges" in *The Anchor Bible*, AB (Garden
City, N.Y.: Doubleday, 1975), p. 72.

statement in 6:10 anticipates the failure that follows in the period of the judges.

C. Summarization of the period (2:11–19)

1. *Reversion to idolatry* (2:11–13)

A cause-effect relationship is seen in 2:10–11. Apostasy followed because the new generation had no acquaintance with the Lord and had not been taught about Him. Israel forsook the Lord and served the Baals. The plural form Baals ("Baalim," KJV) is a general term that denotes all the deities of the Canaanites and is synonymous with the expression "various gods" in 2:12.[2]

The statement in 2:11–12 can be regarded as a summary concerning Israel's apostasy (cf. 3:7, 12; 4:1; 6:1; 10:6; 13:1). There is an added emphasis that the God whom Israel abandoned was the God "who had brought them out of Egypt" (2:12). They abandoned the One who had previously delivered them from bondage in Egypt. That the departure was complete is seen in the statement "They followed and worshiped various gods of the peoples around them" (2:12). The people ignored the earlier prohibitions and warnings concerning intermarriage with the heathen and practicing idolatry (cf. Deut. 4:15–24; 6:14–15; 7:1–11) and thereby invoked the anger of the Lord.

In 2:13 the idolatrous worship of the Israelites is seen in a specific statement: "they forsook him and served Baal and the Ashtoreths." Baal ("lord") was the Canaanite storm-god who ruled the clouds and the rain and therefore denoted reproductive power. He was the consort of the goddess Asherah (also spelled Ashtaroth and other variations). It was thought the sexual union of Baal and Asherah in the heavens resulted in the fertilization and productivity of the crops on earth. The resultant worship was temple prostitution, which was thought to ensure abundant crops through sympathetic magic—doing in the name of worship on earth what Baal and Asherah were believed to be performing in the heavens.[3] The result was a degrading practice in which Israel committed both physical and spiritual adultery against the Lord.

---

[2]Keil and Delitzsch, *Joshua, Judges, Ruth*, p. 268.

[3]For a definitive discussion that traces the development of Baal worship, see M. J. Mulder, "בַּעַל," *Theological Dictionary of the Old Testament*, G. Johannes Botterweck and Helmer Ringgren, eds., John T. Willis, trans., rev. ed., vol. 2 (Grand Rapids: Eerdmans, 1977), pp. 181–200.

2. *Retribution of God* (2:14–15)

These verses give the second aspect of the cycles of oppression and summarize God's judgment on the Israelites during the period of the judges. God chastised the nation for being unfaithful to their covenant with Him. The Lord handed them over to raiders, who plundered them in fulfillment of earlier warnings (Lev. 26:17; Deut. 28:25; Josh. 23:14–16). Since the Israelites had worshiped the gods of the people "around them" (2:12), God subjected them to their enemies "all around" (2:14). This was literally fulfilled as their enemies plundered them on all sides: Aram Naharaim, or Northwest Mesopotamia, from the northeast to the south (3:8); the Moabites from the southeast to the central area (3:12b–14); the Canaanites in the north (4:2); the Midianites in the east and central areas (6:2–6a); Abimelech in the central area (9:7–57); the Ammonites in the east and central area (10:7–9); the Philistines in the west and south (13:1b). Wherever Israel went, the strength of the Lord that had previously brought them victory was now against them so that their enemies continually defeated them. What had previously been true of Israel's enemies was now true of Israel; the chosen people could no longer stand before their enemies (cf. Josh. 10:8).

3. *Liberation through judges* (2:16–19)

These verses further summarize the period of the judges. When the surrounding nations oppressed Israel, the Lord raised up judges who delivered the people from their oppressors (2:16). Although it is not stated here, the Lord responded because of Israel's repentance and cry for help. However, the nation's deliverance was short-lived, usually being limited to the lifetime of the judge. The phrase "they would not listen to their judges" (v. 17) means that the abandonment of idolatry was not permanent, but on the death of the judges the people again reverted to idolatry.

Israel is seen as prostituting herself to other gods (2:17), a practice that was both physical and spiritual. In their idolatrous practices they committed physical adultery, but the sin was magnified inasmuch as the nation had been wedded to the Lord and was seen as unfaithful to her Husband. This picture is particularly observed in Hosea where the prophet's adulterous wife depicts the adulterous nation of Israel (Hos. 1:2; 2:7; 4:15).

When affliction under enemy oppression came, the Lord was moved with pity concerning their cries and delivered them (2:18). The supernatural deliverance is seen in the phrase "he was with the judge." The phrase is reminiscent of God being with Joshua and enabling him to be victorious (Josh. 1:5). Nevertheless, when the judge died the Israelites returned to their idolatrous practices. The statement that "the people returned to ways even more corrupt than those of their fathers" (2:19) suggests an intensifying apostasy.

> A progressive deterioration is revealed, each successive cycle being characterized by a greater descent into apostasy and corruption, and by a more superficial repentance, than the one preceding.[4]

The fathers mentioned in 2:19 were not their godly predecessors, but their corrupt fathers during the period of the judges (cf. vv. 10, 17, 22).[5] The Israelites exceeded their ungodly forefathers in idolatry and in their stubborn refusal to turn from their false worship. The term "stubborn" (v. 19) means hard, referring to people with stiff necks, and is illustrated in the obstinacy of the people in Exodus 32:9; 33:3, 5; 34:9.[6] The figure was taken from a work animal, such as a horse, that would stiffen its neck in resistance to the driver who pulled the rein to the right or left.

D. Infliction on Israel (2:20–3:4)

In the stipulations of the suzerainty-vassal treaty, the vassals were obligated to obey their suzerain. The suzerain, on the other hand, promised to protect and provide for the vassals. Since Israel as the Lord's vassal had failed to live up to her obligations, the Lord as Suzerain would no longer provide protection for the nation. The result was that the Lord would allow the heathen nations to remain in the land; He would no longer drive out the heathen since Israel had broken their obligation in the covenant (Exod. 23:23ff.).[7]

There are several reasons why the Lord did not drive the heathen nations out of the land: 1) God desired to punish Israel for her sin (2:20–21). Israel had been covenanted to the Lord at Sinai (Exod. 19:1–8) and had been warned by the Lord against making any covenant with the inhabitants of the land (Exod. 34:10–17). Since Israel had

---

[4]Cundall and Morris, *Judges and Ruth*, p. 70.
[5]Cooke, *Book of Judges*, p. 31.
[6]Brown, Driver, and Briggs, *Hebrew and English Lexicon*, p. 904.
[7]See Meredith G. Kline, *Treaty of the Great King* (Grand Rapids: Eerdmans, 1963) and George E. Mendenhall, *Law and Covenant in Israel and the Near East* (Pittsburgh: The Biblical Colloquium, 1955).

broken the covenant and intermarried with the pagans, God was punishing the nation in accord with His previous warning (Josh. 23:1-13). 2) God's purpose was to test Israel (2:22). The purpose for the testing is explained in the later half of 2:22: "(to) see whether they will keep the way of the LORD and walk in it as their forefathers did." The testing was designed to discover if the nation would repent of their idolatrous ways and keep the Mosaic covenant. The word "test" (Hebrew, *nasah*) is also used of God testing Abraham's faith at Mount Moriah (Gen. 22:1) and Israel's faith at Marah (Exod. 15:25). In the design of the test the Lord allowed the nations in Canaan to remain; hence, Joshua did not complete the conquest of the land, for God determined to test the faithfulness of the generations that would succeed Joshua (2:23). 3) God wanted to teach warfare to Israel (3:1-2). The generation that arose after the death of Joshua was unfamiliar with warfare. However, the words "to teach warfare" (3:2) do not simply refer to teaching the nation to fight a war. Rather, the nation was to learn that success in warfare would come only through the help of the Lord; therefore, being taught in warfare was synonymous with learning to depend on God to drive out the Canaanites in battle. This valuable lesson had been learned by Joshua's generation, particularly at Jericho and Ai, but also throughout the central, southern, and northern campaigns (Josh. 6:1-12:24).

Among the nations that were allowed to remain in the land were the five rulers of the Philistines (3:3). These reigned in the five city-states of the Philistines: Gath, Gaza, Ekron, Ashdod, and Ashkelon. The Philistines, along with other sea people who are thought to have originated from Crete, invaded Canaan and settled along the seacoast approximately 1200 B.C. However, since the Philistines are mentioned as inhabiting the territory around Beersheba and Gerar (Gen. 21:32; 26:1) during the patriarchal era, Unger concludes that "apparently scattered groups of these people existed for centuries in southwestern Palestine before the arrival of the main body in the first quarter of the twelfth century B.C."[8]

Also remaining entrenched in the land were the Canaanites, the Sidonians, and the Hivites. The term Canaanites appears to be used to denote the inhabitants of the land in general. The Sidonians inhabited the major seaport city-state of Sidon but here probably denotes the

---

[8]Unger, *Archaeology and the Old Testament*, p. 91; see also J. C. Moyer, "Philistines," ZPEB, 4:767-73.

Phoenician people who inhabited the coastal area from Acco northward. The Hivites are generally considered as being the Horites who had established the kingdom of Mitanni in Upper Mesopotamia around 1500 B.C. In Joshua's time they had spread into the land of Canaan and had formed the confederacy of the Gibeonite city-states (Josh. 9:7, 17). The territory of the Hivites is defined as "the Lebanon mountains from Mount Baal Hermon to Lebo Hamath" (3:3). Mount Baal Hermon (later called Mount Hermon) lay north of the territory of Dan. The Hivite territory extended northward to Lebo Hamath, which is probably to be identified with modern Lebweh, fourteen miles north-northeast of Baalbek.

The thought of 2:22 is repeated in 3:4, indicating once more that the Lord left the nations in the land to test Israel to see whether they would obey His commandments.

E. Intermarriage with heathen (3:5-6)

Theses verses indicate the result of Israel's test: they failed to obey the commandments of the Lord (3:4). In addition to incomplete obedience in failing to drive out the pagans and apostatizing into idolatrous worship, Israel also failed through intermarriage with the pagan women. The Lord had earlier warned Israel that they were to destroy their enemies and not intermarry with them, for the nations would turn them away from the Lord to serve idols (Deut. 7: 1-5). The text of 3:5-6 is deliberate in emphasizing Israel's intermingling and intermarriage with the surrounding nations. The Israelites took the pagan daughters in marriage and gave their own daughters to pagan men. The result was a foregone conclusion: "(they) served their gods" (3:6).

For Further Study

1. Read an article on Canaanites, Baal, and Asherah in a Bible dictionary or encyclopedia.

2. Analyze the cause of Israel's reversion to idolatry.

3. Can idolatry be a problem today? How?

4. Why and how may God chasten His people? See 2:20-3:4 and Hebrews 12.

PART TWO:

CONDITIONS DURING
THE PERIOD OF THE JUDGES

Chapter 3

Beginning of the Oppression
(Judges 3:7–31)

The opening chapters of the Book of Judges have provided the causes for the chaotic period; now the writer gives the specific accounts of the idolatrous cycles of Israel's apostasy and deliverance by the judges. Each cycle follows a common pattern: the sin of Israel in lapsing into idolatry; the judgment of the Lord in bringing the nation into bondage; the supplicant cry of repentance; deliverance through a God-appointed judge, and a period of silence prior to the new cycle.

A. First cycle of oppression (3:7–11)

1. Sin: idolatry (3:7)

The statement introducing the first cycle of Israel's apostasy is similar to that which summarized the period of the judges in 2:11–12. Israel did evil in the sight of the Lord; they forgot Him and served the Baals and the Asherahs. The Asherahs (literally, Asheroth, noting the female deity) were frequently symbolized by wooden stakes (Exod. 34:13; Judg. 6:25) or trees (cf. NIV margin of Deut. 16:21).[1] Worshiping the Baals and Asherahs violated the first and second commandments (Exod. 20:3–6).

2. Servitude: Cushan-Rishathaim (3:8)

When the Israelites lapsed into idolatry, the Lord chastised His people by selling them into the hands of Cushan-Rishathaim, king of Aram Naharaim. The designation "sold them into the hands of Cushan-Rishathaim" means the Lord gave Israel entirely into the

---

[1]de Vaux, *Ancient Israel*, pp. 285–86.

power of their enemies and the phrase is frequently seen in Judges (2:14; 3:8; 4:2; 10:7).[2]

The name Cushan-Rishathaim ("double-wicked Cushan") may have been ascribed to the king by his enemies. It is possible that the name actually designates a place, and a number of suggestions have been posited. One suggestion is that he was Cushan rosh Teman, that is, Cushan, the chief of Teman, a town in northern Edom. This solution, however, necessitates suggesting that Aram is a scribal error and should read Edom. A better suggestion is that Aram Naharaim (frequently translated Mesopotamia), which means "Syria of the two rivers," refers to the land in Upper Mesopotamia between the Orontes and Euphrates Rivers.[3]

Cushan-Rishathaim subjugated the Israelites for eight years—sufficient time to extend his influence throughout the land to the south from where Othniel, the deliverer, would come.

3. *Supplication* (3:9a)

The result of the oppression now fulfilled a major purpose of the Lord—the oppressor was designed to bring the nation to repentance, showing them their absolute need of trusting the Lord for their deliverance. The cry of repentance occurs frequently in Israel's sinning cycles (3:9, 15; 4:3; 6:6-7; 10:10).

4. *Salvation: Othniel* (3:9b–10)

The Lord responded to the penitential prayer of His people by sending them a "deliverer," or savior, who would rescue them from the power of their oppressor. The Hebrew verb has a variety of meanings. In some contexts the term refers to heroic men saving the nation in war (Judg. 3:9, 15, 31; 6:15; 10:1; 1 Sam. 10:27; Jer. 14:8; Hos. 13:10), but the term is also used as a title for Messiah (Isa. 19:20) and God (Isa. 43:11; 45:15, 21).[4] There is a sense, then, in which the work of each judge in delivering Israel prefigures the work of Messiah in ultimately saving Israel at the end of the age. The name Jesus ("Yahweh saves" or "delivers") is derived from the same root word as the word "deliverer" in 3:9.[5]

---

[2]Brown, Driver, and Briggs, *Hebrew and English Lexicon*, p. 569.
[3]Wiseman, "Mesopotamia," NBD, p. 811.
[4]Brown, Driver, and Briggs, *Hebrew and English Lexicon*, p 446.
[5]Merrill F. Unger and William White, Jr., eds., *Nelson's Expository Dictionary of the Old Testament* (Nashville: Thomas Nelson, 1980), pp. 93–94.

The first deliverer the Lord raised up was Othniel, the younger brother of Caleb. He also conquered Debir and received Caleb's daughter in marriage (1:11–15).

The key to Othniel's success is provided in the phrase "the Spirit of the LORD came upon him" (3:10), a common expression in the Book of Judges (6:34; 11:29; 13:25; 14:6, 19; 15:14). Charles Ryrie suggests there is no great distinction between the Spirit's indwelling and the Spirit coming on the individual, "except that the idea of coming upon seems to imply the temporary and transitory character of the Spirit's relationship to Old Testament saints."[6] The temporary ministry of the Spirit is seen in that the Spirit came on an individual for a specific task. It is reasonable to assume that when the task had been carried out, the Spirit was no longer on the individual as He had been previously.

An examination of the pertinent passages indicates the purpose of the Spirit's ministry and the uniqueness of the individuals on whom the Spirit came. The Spirit came on Othniel for the purpose of conquering Cushan-Rishathaim (3:10). The Spirit came on Gideon for the purpose of defeating the Midianites (6:34). The Spirit came on Jephthah to defeat the Ammonites (11:29). It is significant to note that Jephthah was the son of a prostitute (11:1), grew up in his mother's idolatrous surroundings, and gathered adventurous men around him (11:3). Different terms are used to describe the Spirit coming on Samson to defeat the Philistines (14:4): "the Spirit of the LORD began to stir him" (13:25); "the Spirit of the LORD came upon him in power" (14:6, 19). Outside the Book of Judges the Spirit is recorded as coming on Balaam, an unbeliever (Num. 24:2). "An evaluation of these texts shows that all involved empowerment for a physical activity. None of them had to do with salvation from sin in any sense,"[7] nor did the empowering have anything to do with the spiritual condition of the person—note Samson, Jephthah, and Balaam. The significant conclusion is that in the Old Testament economy the Holy Spirit came on individuals for service, but He also left them (1 Sam. 11:6; 16:14). In the church age the Holy Spirit indwells His people forever (John 14:16; Eph. 4:30).

---

[6]Charles Caldwell Ryrie, *The Holy Spirit* (Chicago: Moody Press, 1965), pp. 41–42.

[7]Leon Wood, *The Holy Spirit in the Old Testament* (Grand Rapids: Zondervan, 1976), p. 41. The distinctive work of the Holy Spirit in the differing economies merits study. For a comprehensive treatment see John F. Walvoord, *The Holy Spirit* (Grand Rapids: Zondervan, 1958).

5. *Silence: forty years* (3:11)

Following Othniel's conquest of Cushan-Rishathaim, the land had peace for forty years. The forty years probably has reference to one generation and suggests the failure of the people to transmit God's truth to succeeding generations (cf. Deut. 6:4–9). Only once in the seven cycles did the land have peace for more than one generation (cf. 3:11—forty years; 3:30—eighty years; 5:31—forty years; 8:28—forty years; 10:2–3—forty-five years; 12:7–14—thirty-one years; 16:31—twenty years).

B. Second Cycle of Oppression (3:12–31)

1. *Sin: apostasy* (3:12a)

In beginning the record of the second cycle of Israel's apostasy, the author emphasizes the deepening depravity of the nation by the phrase "once again." The Hebrew text uses a verb that literally means "to add" and here means to "do again" or "more"[8] (cf. 4:1; 10:6; 13:1).

2. *Servitude: Eglon* (3:12b–14)

Since the Israelites apostatized again, the Lord delivered them into the power of Eglon, king of Moab. The Moabites, who were descendants of Lot through the incestuous relationship with his daughter (Gen. 19:30–38), occupied the territory between the Arnon and Zered rivers. To strengthen his hand, Eglon allied himself with the Ammonites and Amalekites (3:13). The Ammonites were the northern neighbors of Moab and related to the Moabites in that they were descendants of Lot through his incestuous relationship with his younger daughter (Gen. 19:38). The Amalekites, a nomadic people who occupied the territory south of Beersheba, were bitter enemies of Israel. Although defeated at Rephidim (Exod. 17:8–13), they continued to attack and harass Israel after the Exodus (Deut. 25:17–19).

In leading the attack against the Israelites, Eglon entered the land through the same valley that Joshua had used and attacked the City of Palms, that is, Jericho (cf. 1:16). Apparently Israel had reoccupied the city of Jericho after its destruction but had not fortified it because of the curse (Josh. 6:26). The Moabite alliance held the Israelites in subjugation for eighteen years (3:14).

---

[8]Brown, Driver, and Briggs, *Hebrew and English Lexicon*, pp. 414–15.

3. Supplication (3:15a)

Being held under the domination of Eglon along the Jordan Valley, the Israelites cried to the Lord for deliverance.

4. Salvation: Ehud (3:15b–29)

a) Deception of Ehud (3:15b–20)

Ehud, the deliverer, was a descendant of Gera (1 Chron. 8:3) and thus a Benjamite. Apparently there was a tendency among some of the Benjamites to be left-handed (cf. 20:16 where seven hundred are described as left-handed). The Hebrew phraseology is interesting: "a left-handed man" is, literally, "a man bound in his right hand." This does not mean, as some have suggested, that he was crippled in his right hand, but rather that it was considered peculiar to be left-handed.

Eglon forced the conquered Israelites to pay "tribute" (3:15), a practice commonly used by conquering nations (cf. 2 Sam. 8:2, 6). The word tribute (Hebrew, *minchah*) means "gift, tribute, offering"[9] and was frequently used to designate an offering made to God, whether grain or animals (Gen. 4:3–5; Lev. 2:1, 4, 13–15; 23:16–17 et al.)

> This probably was an annual tribute that the Moabites had laid on the Israelites. Tribute paying was customary in such situations, and it was normally required that the person bringing it be important among his people. The king who imposed the tribute was made to feel more important when a leader was forced to humble himself in bringing it personally.[10]

Ehud's preparations for bringing Eglon the tribute included hiding an eighteen-inch sword (actually a dagger) on his right thigh under his clothing. If he were searched, it was unlikely that the searcher would examine his right thigh, for a right-handed man normally would grasp a sword from his left thigh. It is probable the sword had no cross shaft and thus could easily be concealed. Armed with the deadly weapon, Ehud prepared to bring Israel's annual tribute payment to Eglon at Jericho. The parenthetical phrase "who was a very fat man" anticipates the events that follow (cf. 3:22).

The tribute itself may have been gold, produce from the land, or other items requiring assistance to be transported. Having delivered the tribute to Jericho, Ehud was returning with his men when he sent them away while he alone turned back at Gilgal. This would not arouse

[9]Brown, Driver, and Briggs, *Hebrew and English Lexicon*, p. 585.
[10]Wood, *Distressing Days*, p. 173.

suspicion among the Moabites.[11] On returning Ehud announced that he had a message from God for the king (3:19). Having aroused the king's curiosity, Ehud was able to secure a private audience with Eglon, who dismissed his attendants with a shout.

Ehud approached king Eglon, who was in the upper room of his summer palace (3:20). The king's upper room was in a corner of the roof and had many latticed windows, enabling the cooling breezes to freely enter. It was a comfortable location for a private interview. Ehud exclaimed, "I have a message from God for you" (v. 20), and Eglon rose from his seat in anticipation to receive the message.

b) *Destruction of Eglon* (3:21–25)

Since Ehud was left-handed, Eglon failed to notice his visitor's movement. Ehud drew his sword with his left hand and quickly thrust it into Eglon's stomach. The attacker was unable to withdraw the sword because fat instantly swallowed up the whole weapon, including the handle. The phrase translated "(it) came out his back" presents a difficulty. The words could refer to either the sword passing entirely through Eglon or may refer to excrement being forced out of the king as a natural result of a wound in the abdomen.[12]

As Ehud left he shut and bolted the door behind him (3:23). By delaying the discovery of Eglon's body, Ehud gained sufficient time to escape. When the servants came to investigate and saw the doors of the upper room closed, they thought the king was relieving himself and did not enter. The phrase translated "relieving himself" literally reads "covering his feet," a euphemism for elimination (cf. 1 Sam. 24:3).

The servants waited until they were embarrassed and then took a key and unlocked the door (3:25). On entering they found their lord lying dead.

c) *Deliverance of Israel* (3:26–29)

The delay in discovering Eglon's body enabled Ehud to escape. He passed by the idols at Gilgal and came to the hill country of Ephraim; here he quickly marshaled an army, using a trumpet to summon men to battle. Since the Ephraimites had felt the effects of the oppression the most, they eagerly responded to the call. It appears Ehud made a circuitous trip through the hill country to gather his warriors.[13] Speed

---

[11]Pfeiffer, "Judges," WBC, p. 240.

[12]George Foot Moore, *A Critical and Exegetical Commentary on Judges* in *The International Critical Commentary*, ICC (New York: Charles Scribner's Sons, 1906), p. 97; Pfeiffer, *WBC*, p. 240.

[13]Aharoni and Avi-Yonah, *The Macmillan Bible Atlas*, p. 54.

was now of the utmost importance to take advantage of the Moabite confusion following the assassination of their king.

The Ephraimites' attack cut off the enemy's escape route, for Ehud's men guarded the shallow part of the Jordan River where the Moabites would have attempted to cross into their own land (3:28). The Ephraimites struck down about ten thousand vigorous and strong Moabites (v. 29). The Hebrew word for "vigorous" also is the word for "fat"[14] and suggests the Moabites may have been like their king.

5. Silence: eighty years (3:30–31)

Following the Moabite defeat, the nation had rest for eighty years (3:30).

The next judge, Shamgar, struck down six hundred Philistines with an oxgoad. Shamgar appears as a minor judge, which leads Cundall to suggest "he may not have been a judge after the usual pattern but just a warrior who effected this one local stroke of valour against a nation who afterwards became Israel's principal oppressor."[15] However, Leon Wood has demonstrated from the biblical text that Shamgar should be classified as a judge.[16] His accomplishment in killing six hundred Philistines is one line of evidence.

The name Shamgar is Hurrian, indicating that he was probably a Canaanite convert to Israel—but the name also attests to the intermingling of Israel with the Canaanites.

The oxgoad, the weapon used by Shamgar to defeat the Philistines, was a sharp, pointed stick used to urge on an animal. It was about eight feet long and had a sharp metal tip on one end so it could be used as a spear in warfare. The other end had a blade like a chisel for use in cleaning a plow.

The book of Judges records that Israel was afflicted by the Philistines during the time of Shamgar (3:31), after the time of Jair (10:6–7), prior to the time of Samson (13:1), and during the time of Samson (13:24–16:31).

For Further Study

1. Read articles in a Bible encyclopedia or dictionary on Mesopotamia and Moab.

---

[14]Brown, Driver, and Briggs, *Hebrew and English Lexicon*, p. 1032.
[15]Cundall and Morris, *Judges and Ruth*, p. 80.
[16]Wood, *Distressing Days*, p. 176.

2. How important is the relationship of chastisement to repentance?

3. Study the contrasting ministry of the Holy Spirit in the Old Testament and in the New Testament (cf. Judg. 3:10; 6:34; 11:29; 1 Sam. 11:6; 16:14; John 14:16; Rom. 8:9; Eph. 1:13; 4:30).

Chapter 4

Third Cycle of Oppression
(Judges 4:1–5:31)

The third cycle of Israel's oppression involved Jabin, king of the great northern city of Hazor, who oppressed the northern Israelite tribes. The narrative of Israel's conquest under the leadership of Deborah and Barak is described in chapter 4, while the song of triumph is recorded in chapter 5.

A. Sin: apostasy (4:1)

The importance of the judge in guiding the people is seen in this verse; as long as Ehud was alive, the people remained loyal to the Lord, but when Ehud died they apostatized.

> The circumstantial clause, "when Ehud was dead," places the falling away of the Israelites from God in direct causal connection with the death of Ehud on the one hand, and the deliverance of Israel into the power of Jabin on the other, and clearly indicates that as long as Ehud lived he kept the people from idolatry (cf. chap. ii. 18, 19), and defended Israel from hostile oppressions.[1]

B. Servitude: Jabin (4:2)

The oppressor who subjugated the northern tribes was Jabin, king of Hazor, a kingdom that Israel had previously defeated under Joshua (Josh. 11: 1–11). Some commentators suggest these two accounts refer to the same event and the writer has confused them. More reasonable, however, is the suggestion that Jabin was a dynastic title for the Canaanite kings of Hazor. Hazor had previously been destroyed and burned by the Israelites, but they had not occupied the city. Because of the strategic location, the Canaanites rebuilt the city and once more

---

[1]Keil and Delitzsch, *Joshua, Judges, Ruth*, pp. 300–301.

occupied it. Kenneth Kitchen has provided sound evidence to indicate the contrast between Jabin I and Jabin II.[2] In the Judges account the emphasis is on Jabin as king of Canaan (4:2, 23, 24 twice) more than as king of Hazor (vv. 2, 17). Moreover, the emphasis in Judges is on the strength of Sisera rather than the strength of Hazor.

Located five miles southwest of Lake Huleh, was the major city of its day. The site of Hazor was identified as Tell el-Qedah by John Garstang in 1926, but was not excavated until 1955 by Yigael Yadin. The city consisted of the tell proper, plus some twenty-five acres rising 165 feet above the road and 170 acres of level plateau. The probable population of the city was forty thousand, which was very large for that day.[3]

Jabin's army commander, Sisera, lived in Harosheth Haggoyim ("Harosheth of the Gentiles"). The site is uncertain, but one possibility is Tell el-Harbaj overlooking the Kishon River as it flows northwest around Mount Carmel. The normally shallow river could readily flood at this narrow passage of less than a mile.[4] Others identify the site as Tell Amar, ten miles northwest of Meggido.

C. Supplication (4:3)

Israel cried to the Lord for help because Jabin had military superiority with nine hundred iron chariots and used his power to oppress Israel for twenty years. The chariots were particularly suitable for combat on the plains and probably explain Jabin's control of the Esdraelon Valley.

D. Salvation: Deborah and Barak (4:4–5:31a)

1. Deliberation of Deborah and Barak (4:4–11)

Deborah is the only woman mentioned in the Book of Judges as having served as a judge in Israel. A woman normally held a subordinate place in Israelite society. The fact that Israel had a woman lead them in battle probably says as much concerning the disruption of Israelite society as it does that a woman could lead them to victory. This appears to be emphasized in the account as well. After Deborah

---

[2]K. A. Kitchen, *Ancient Orient and Old Testament* (Chicago: Inter-Varsity Press, 1966), pp. 67–69. *The Macmillan Bible Atlas* confuses the events of Joshua 11 and Judges 4. Cf. Aharoni and Avi-Yonah, *The Macmillan Bible Atlas*, pp. 46–47.

[3]See also John Garstang, *Joshua-Judges* (Grand Rapids: Kregel, 1979), pp. 183–90, 381–83; Yigael Yadin, "Hazor," *Archaeology* in *Israel Pocket Library* (Jerusalem: Keter Books, 1974). pp. 92–99.

[4]Garstang, *Joshua-Judges*, pp. 296–98; Wood, *Distressing Days*, p. 184.

prophesied that God would deliver Jabin's army into the hands of Israel, Barak was afraid to go (4:8). Only after Deborah agreed to go with Barak would he consent. Deborah seemed to emphasize the cowardice of Barak and the entire nation at this point when she reminded Barak that a woman, not he, would receive credit for the victory (v. 9).

Deborah is described as being both a prophetess and a judge. The term prophet (Hebrew, *nabhi*) emphasizes the prophetic office and indicates a person who received a message directly from God and conveyed it to the people. That person was a spokesman for God.[5] Deborah had that ability and probably on the basis of that ability was called on to judge Israel (cf. Miriam, Exod. 15:20, and Huldah, 2 Kings 22:14).

Deborah held court under a palm named after her that was between Bethel and Ramah. She apparently heard the difficult cases that the lower courts were unable to solve (cf. Deut. 16:18; 17:8). God revealed to Deborah that He would deliver Israel from the oppression of Jabin, whereupon Deborah summoned Barak, who was from Kedesh in Naphtali (4:6). The choice was a logical one since Barak was from the territory that would have been affected directly by the oppression of Jabin. Barak was instructed to gather ten thousand men at Mount Tabor, which bordered the three tribal territories of Zebulun, Naphtali, and Issachar. God explained through Deborah that he would lure Sisera and his troops to the Kishon River, ten miles west of Mount Tabor. In ordinary circumstances the Kishon was only a trickle; however, following a rainstorm the river became a swollen torrent. The statement "I will...give him into your hands" (4:7) anticipates the outcome (5:21).

Barak expressed his unwillingness to go up alone to fight Sisera, agreeing to do so only if Deborah would accompany him (4:8). Perhaps because of his timidity Barak needed the reassurance of the prophetess; in any case, Deborah announced the consequence of Barak's lack of faith: a woman would take credit for the victory (v. 9). The prophetic statement was fulfilled in Jael (v. 21).

Deborah accompanied Barak to Kedesh, north of Hazor, where Barak summoned ten thousand men from the northern tribes of Zebulun and Naphtali (4:10); others came to help fight (see comments at

<hr>

[5]See Edward J. Young, *My Servants The Prophets* (Grand Rapids: Eerdmans, 1952), pp. 56–75; Hobart E. Freeman, *An Introduction to the Old Testament Prophets* (Chicago: Moody Press, 1968), pp. 36–50.

5:12–18). The statement in 4:11 is parenthetical and anticipates 4:17. It explains why the Kenites, who were normally identified with Judah (1:16), were living so far north.

2. Defeat of the Canaanites (4:12–16)

Sisera was informed that Israel had mustered their troops at Mount Tabor, whereupon Sisera moved his army of nine hundred chariots southeast to the Kishon River. This movement is not entirely understood; perhaps Gray's comment provides the solution.

> This movement, which involved a detour to the river, is hard to understand unless a diversion had been created towards Megiddo to lure Sisera into chosen terrain, . . . Perhaps a rumour was disseminated that the Israelites intended to attack Megiddo or Taanach to divert Sisera south of the Kishon between the river and the mountains to restrict the movement of his chariots.[6]

Having viewed the valley and Sisera's troop movements, Deborah ordered the attack. Barak and his men rushed down from Mount Tabor against Sisera and his forces (4:14). It is uncertain where the battle actually took place since the place is not stated. From Deborah's victory song it appears that the Israelites rushed westward and that the battle occurred near Megiddo and Taanach (cf. 5:19).

It is possible that Deborah's command to attack came when she saw the approaching storm—an unusual phenomenon at this time of year (probably the dry season) since Sisera would not have ventured forth with his chariots in the rainy season.[7] The Valley of Esdraelon would have been ideally suited for Sisera's chariots in the dry season, but following a rainstorm the chariots were a definite liability.

Although the text simply states that the Lord routed Sisera (4:15), Deborah's song indicates a rainstorm was the means the Lord used in giving Israel the victory (5:19–21). The rainstorm softened the marshes which in turn rendered the chariots useless; moreover, as Sisera's men fled along the narrowing valley toward Harosheth Haggoyim, the torrent of water and mud swept Sisera's army away, enabling the Israelites to gain the victory with the sword (4:16).

Since the Lord is seen as the God of the thunderstorm (Ps. 18:9–15), and Baal was held to be the god of the rainstorm, the victory may be interpreted as both a national and religious judgment on the Canaanite people.

---

[6]Gray, "Joshua, Judges and Ruth," p. 271.
[7]Cundall and Morris, *Judges and Ruth*, pp. 86–87.

3. Death of Sisera (4:17-22)

The utter confusion of the Canaanite army is seen in that Sisera's escape route was different from that of his army. Having abandoned his chariot, Sisera fled on foot to the tent of Jael, the wife of Heber the Kenite. Evidently Sisera assumed he would be safe there since the Kenites had friendly relations with the king of Hazor (4:17). As a fugitive from Israel, Sisera not only was tired in mind and body but was desperately in need of rest. Jael provided Sisera hospitality in the normal custom:

> According to the usages of nomadic people, the duty of receiving the stranger in the sheikh's absence devolves on his wife; and the moment the stranger is admitted into the tent, his claim to be defended or concealed from his pursuers is established.[8]

Jael hid Sisera in her tent and "put a covering over him" (4:18). The place of concealment probably was "the screened quarter of the women, which would give Sisera a sense of false security and, from Jael's point of view, hide an embarrassing quest."[9]

Sisera'a request for water (4:19) was designed not only to alleviate his thirst, but was also a plea for security.

> It is an ancient, oriental practice, common to all Bedouins, Arabs, and the inhabitants of deserts in general, that whoever has eaten or drunk anything in the tent, is received into the peace of the house. The Arab's mortal enemy slumbers securely in the tent of his adversary, if he have drunk with him.[10]

The text emphasizes that Jael brought him milk instead of water (4:19; 5:25), and this has led some to suggest the milk was a mild sedative that enabled Jael to carry out her deed.[11] Curdled milk was viewed as a refreshing drink and was commonly used. As a final precaution Sisera requested that Jael stand in the doorway of the tent to divert any pursuers (4:20).

When Sisera was asleep Jael took a wooden mallet and tent peg and quietly approached Sisera. Placing the peg at Sisera'a temple, she struck it with such force that it was driven through his head into the ground. Jael was adept at using the mallet to drive tent pegs since women had the responsibility of pitching the tents. Sisera died in-

---

[8]Robert Jamieson, "Judges," *A Commentary Critical, Experimental, and Practical on the Old and New Testaments*, vol. 2 (Grand Rapids: Eerdmans, 1946), p. 82.
[9]Gray, *Joshua, Judges and Ruth*, p. 273.
[10]Cassel, "The Book of Judges," *Lange's*, p. 87.
[11]Boling, "Judges", AB, pp. 97-98, 114.

stantly. As Barak approached Jael led him into her tent and revealed her deed to the Israelite commander. The prophecy of Deborah was fulfilled (4:9) and Barak was deprived of a personal victory. Sisera's ignominious death was considered shameful because he died at the hands of a woman (cf. 9:54).

4. *Destruction of Jabin* (4:23-24)

With the defeat of Sisera, Hazor's power was broken. The indication, however, is that the final conquest of Hazor nonetheless took some time. It is noteworthy that God was ultimately given credit for the victory.

5. *Deborah's Song* (5:1-31a)

Deborah's victory over Sisera is described in two forms: in prose in chapter 4 and in poetry in chapter 5. It is generally agreed that this magnificent descriptive poem is contemporaneous with the events.

a) *Exaltation of the Lord* (5:1-5)

While both Deborah and Barak sang the song of triumph, the text indicates that Deborah was the author of the song (5:7, 12). The song opens with a call to praise the Lord for the response of the leaders and the people of Israel in volunteering for battle against the enemy (v. 2). There are translation difficulties in verse 2, but when rendered as "When the princes in Israel take the lead," the poetic form of synonymous parallelism is preserved.[12] In this poetic form the second line restates the thought of the first line in different words.

The song enjoins the surrounding kings to pay attention to the mighty acts of Israel's God. Climactic or stairlike parallelism is observed in 5:3 where a second line repeats and expands the thought of the previous line: The words "I will make music to the LORD, the God of Israel" develop the thought of "I will sing to the LORD, I will sing." Deborah recounts the Lord's provision for Israel in the desert wanderings as He came forth from Edom, the vicinity where the Lord first revealed Himself to Israel (Exod. 19). The more specific statement refers to Sinai in 5:5. The allusion to the Lord's initial meeting with Israel (Exod. 19:16-18) is expressed in the statement "The mountains quaked before the LORD, the One of Sinai" (5:5). On this occasion the

---

[12]For an explanation of Hebrew poetry see A. Berkeley Mickelsen, *Interpreting the Bible* (Grand Rapids: Eerdmans, 1963), pp. 323-37; and Harrison, *Introduction to the Old Testament*, pp. 965-75.

Lord came forth in response to Israel's cry and defeated the forces of Sisera.

b) *Ecstasy of the people* (5:6–11)

The text indicates that Shamgar the judge served Israel briefly during this time; moreover, he had a localized judgeship during which Israel was oppressed by Jabin. The Canaanites had subjugated Israel to the extent of controlling the major roads; as a result Israel had to travel the "winding paths" (5:6; literally, "crooked paths"). Because of fear of the Canaanites, travelers had deserted the main roads. Peasants too became afraid of the Canaanites and left their small unprotected villages and agricultural life for the security of the walled towns and cities (v. 7).

The oppression continued until Deborah arose! Israel had turned to idolatry and war had resulted. The oppressive conflict reached to the gates of the cities, and the Israelites were unable to properly defend themselves since not one among forty thousand had a shield or spear (5:8). Yet there were those who were faithful in the time of crisis and volunteered for battle, and so Deborah expresses her gratitude (v. 9). Now Deborah calls for all the people to sing and be thankful to God for the victory over the Canaanites. She calls to the rich—those who ride the prized white donkeys that were expensive due to their rarity; she calls to the nobles who sit on expensive rugs and the common people who walk along the road. All are to praise God! Even at the wells and watering places people would praise the Lord, recounting His mighty deeds.

> Near the wells and fountains the robber and assassin commonly took his station; and in time of war the enemy placed their ambush there, because the flocks and herds, in which the wealth of the country chiefly consisted, were twice every day collected to those places, and might be seized with less danger when the shepherds were busily engaged in drawing water;…The wells, which are at a little distance from the towns in the East, are, in unsettled times, places of danger. But in peace they are scenes of pleasant and joyous resort. [13]

c) *Endeavors of the tribes* (5:12–18)

Deborah and Barak are pictured as awakening, being aroused to the task of leading an army against their oppressors. As Deborah and Barak appealed to the people, a remnant arose to battle the oppressors (5:13). Many responded: the Ephraimites who came from the central hill country previously occupied by the Amalekites, the Benjamites who

---

[13]Jamieson, "Judges," pp. 84–85.

lived below Ephraim, the captains of Makir (the descendant of Manasseh, Num. 26:29, here referring to the western half of Manasseh), the commanders of the oppressed area of Zebulun, and the people of Issachar.

Deborah and Barak rebuked those who refused to respond (5:15b–18). The tribe of Reuben failed to participate perhaps because they were a considerable distance from the oppression of Jabin. Although the Reubenites had second thoughts, they remained in their isolated, pastoral setting. Gilead—the eastern tribes of Gad and the half-tribe of Manasseh—also refused to cross the Jordan and assist in the battle (v. 17). The tribe of Dan was more interested in their commerce (cf. port city of Joppa, Josh. 19:46) than in assisting their brothers. Asher also remained at his seacoast home, refusing to participate (5:17). The section concludes with a contrast between the tribes that refused to help and those who did (v. 18). The army included ten thousand men of Zebulun and Naphtali who risked their lives in fighting Jabin (4:10).

d) *Echo of the heavens* (5:19–23)

The alliance of the Canaanite kings fought at Taanach in anticipation of the spoils of war but were empty-handed after the battle. The reason for their failure is described in verses 20–21. "From the heavens the stars fought" is a reference to the intervention of God in behalf of Israel. God fought for Israel by sending a torrent of rain. The downpour swelled the Kishon River, which swept away the Canaanites at they fled their chariots (v. 21). The Canaanites' frantic flight is vividly pictured in verse 22 by the repetitious word "galloping." The town of Meroz was cursed for its failure to assist the Israelites in preventing the Canaanites' escape (v. 23).

e) *Execution of Sisera* (5:24–31a)

Jael's execution of Sisera is recounted in verses 24–27 where her bravery stands in contrast to the cowardice of the people of Meroz. The section concludes by picturing Sisera's mother waiting for the general's return (v. 28). When he failed to return she was comforted by her attending ladies, who suggested that he was dividing the spoils of war: a slave-girl or two and colorful embroidered garments!

The statement "So may all your enemies perish, O LORD!" (5:31) is similar to statements in the imprecatory psalms (cf. Pss. 35; 69; 83; 101 et al.) that call for the destuction of God's enemies. By contrast, those who love the Lord enjoy His strength and blessing.

E. Silence: forty years (5:31b)

Following the defeat of Sisera and the destruction of Hazor, the land had peace for forty years—only one generation.

For Further Study

1. Study a Bible map of the period of Judges and locate the following: Hazor, Kishon River, Harosheth, Mount Tabor, Taanach, Megiddo, and the tribes mentioned in chapters 4 and 5.

2. Read articles in a Bible dictionary or encyclopedia on Hazor, Kishon River, and Mount Tabor.

3. Was Jael justified in killing Sisera? Explain.

4. Study the victory over the armies of Jabin in the light of human responsibility and divine sovereignty.

5. Develop a character study of Barak. What were his strengths? his weaknesses?

Chapter 5

Fourth Cycle of Oppression
(Judges 6:1–8:32)

The fourth cycle of oppression occurred as Midianite invaders came against Israel from the southeast. The attack resulted in extreme humiliation for the Israelites, who were forced to hide in caves. The Lord delivered Israel through Gideon to whom more space is devoted than to any other personality in the Book of Judges.

A. Sin: apostasy (6:1)

Following forty years of peace Israel again turned from the Lord, whereupon He gave His people into the hands of the Midianites. The oppressors were related to Israel, being descendants of Midian, a son of Abraham by Keturah (Gen. 25:1–2). They were a nomadic people who moved about according to the availability of pasture for their herds and flocks. The Midianites evidently were a prosperous people, for when Israel conquered them (Num. 31:32–34) the spoils were great: 675,000 sheep, 72,000 cattle, and 61,000 donkeys. The mention of donkeys in Numbers 31 indicates the Midianites used them as their means of transportation at that time rather than camels. Later, in the invasion recorded in Judges 6 and 7, the Midianites used camels in transportation and warfare.

Originally, the Midianites made their home east of the Gulf of Aqabah, but their nomadic lifestyle took them to other areas, principally east of the Dead Sea and south of the Jabbok River.

B. Servitude: Midian (6:2–6a)

1. *Persecution of Israel* (6:2)

The Midianite oppression forced the Israelites into unusual forms of living: "the Israelites prepared shelters for themselves in mountain clefts, caves and strongholds" (6:2). Because the Hebrew word translated "shelters" is a *hapax legomenon* it is difficult to precisely determine its meaning. "The root *nhr* suggests a ravine, or river valley; hence the *dens* are clefts or defiles in the mountains caused by river erosion, which make excellent hiding places."[1] There were also many natural caves and dens in Israel and, in addition, the Israelites made other caves in which to hide. The purpose for this was twofold: (1) To hide from the raids of the Midianites in time of war; (2) To conceal their produce from the marauders. This is further explained in 6:4–5.

2. *Destruction of crops* (6:3–6a)

The invaders were a coalition of three warring parties: the Midianites, the Amalekites (see comments on 3:13), and "other eastern peoples" (literally, "the sons of the east"), who were nomads from the Syrian desert.

The Midianites traveled north from the Gulf of Aqabah into the Trans-Jordan region, crossing the Jordan as far north as the Valley of Jezreel (6:33), yet penetrating the land as far south and east as Gaza (v. 4). In their invasions the Midianites temporarily settled in the land, using the pasture for their own herds while plundering the produce. The loss of crops and livestock to the Midianites made life extremely difficult for the Israelites in the succeeding years.

The Midianites came like "swarms of locusts" (6:5), an apt and terrifying description.[2] The invaders had a decided advantage due to their possession of camels. Many suggest that these incursions constituted the first full-scale deployment of camels as a major factor in warfare. A camel could carry four hundred pounds in addition to its rider and could readily travel three or four days, and even a week, without drinking. In ordinary travel a camel could average twenty-eight miles a day, but with only a rider could travel as much as one hundred miles in a day. The broad, cushioned hoofs made the animal highly effective in various types of terrain.[3] There was little Israel could do to stop the marauders.

C. Supplication (6:6b–10)

1. *Petition* (6:6b)

The consequences of disobedience stated in Deuteronomy 28:43

---

[1]Boling, "Judges," AB, p. 122.
[2]For a vivid description of a locust plague, see John D. Whiting, "Jerusalem's Locust Plague," *National Geographic* XXVIII (December, 1915), pp. 511–50.
[3]G. S. Cansdale, "Camel," ZPEB, 1:695–99.

were realized in the experience of the Israelites during the annual Midianite incursions. God's people were brought very low, and in their desperate condition they cried to the Lord for deliverance.

2. *Admonition* (6:7–10)

Before the deliverance was effected, the Lord sent an unnamed prophet among the Israelites to remind them of why the oppression had come. The divine rebuke parallels the admonition in 2:1–5. Through the prophet God reminded Israel of His faithfulness in delivering the nation from previous oppression: "I brought you up out of Egypt, . . . I snatched you from the power of Egypt . . . I drove them from before you and (I) gave you their land" (6:8–9). While the Lord had been faithful to Israel, they had been unfaithful to Him by worshiping the gods of the Amorites (6:10) in violation of the first commandment of the Decalogue (Exod. 20:3).

D. Salvation: Gideon (6:11–8:27)

1. *Call of Gideon* (6:11–24)

a) *Manifestation of the angel* (6:11–14)

Gideon's call as a deliverer began with a visit by the angel of the Lord. The angel's appearance was a theophany since the text makes it clear that the angel of the Lord is synonymous with the Lord (cf. 6:11, 14).

The angel of the Lord appeared to Gideon at Ophrah, whose location is uncertain. A possible site is et-Taiyibeh, eight miles northwest of Beth Shan. The mention of the oak is variously seen in the Old Testament as idolatrous worship (cf. 1 Kings 14:23; 2 Kings 17:10; Isa. 1:29; 57:5), or genuine worship (Josh. 24:26) as in Ophrah, which became a worship center.[4]

When the angel of the Lord approached Gideon, he was threshing wheat in a wine press—a most unusual procedure! This action helps explain 6:2; the Israelites were forced to hide themselves and their produce to prevent pillaging by the raiders. Normally wheat was beat out on an elevated, exposed place where the wind could separate the wheat from the chaff; now the Israelites had to conceal themselves and were beating out their wheat in wine presses. It was not an efficient process, and such a procedure indicates the smallness of Israel's harvest.

---

[4]de Vaux, *Ancient Israel*, pp. 278, 306.

Perhaps there is a point of humor as the Lord addressed Gideon as the "mighty warrior" (6:12). Surely Gideon felt anything but valiant at this point; he was hiding from the Midianites! On the other hand the narrator may want to convey that the Lord saw potential in Gideon and was addressing him as a "mighty warrior" because of what he would become through divine empowerment.

The statement "The LORD is with you" (6:12) anticipates Israel's deliverance through Gideon. Gideon could not conceive of the Lord's presence in view of Israel's suffering; no miraculous deliverance from the Midianite oppression seemed possible. The Lord's response was to commission Gideon to deliver Israel, saying, "Go in the strength you have and save Israel out of Midian's hand. Am I not sending you?" (6:14). The strength of Gideon was not now an ordinary strength, for the Lord had just declared that He was with Gideon. The warrior would now go forth in the strength of the Lord. The question "Am I not sending you?" is reminiscent of the Lord commissioning Moses (Exod. 3:12).

b) *Modesty of Gideon* (6:15–18)

Gideon immediately objected to the commissioning, suggesting he was inadequate for the task due to two factors: (1) his "clan" (usually translated "thousands") was the weakest in all Manasseh; (2) he was the youngest in his home. Gideon considered himself the least of the least! How could there be any hope of success? How could he possibly achieve anything? The Lord had surely made a mistake!

Was Gideon suffering from inferiority or was he a truly humble man? The text suggests he was fearful (6:27). Perhaps there was a combination of inferiority and humility. The Lord assured Gideon of His presence, a requisite for those who will do great exploits for God (cf. Exod. 3:12; Josh. 1:5).

To allay his fear and reassure himself that God had actually called him, Gideon asked for a "sign" (6:17). It was a significant request, for Gideon was asking for a miraculous confirmation. The Hebrew word for "sign" denotes a miracle as a pledge or attestation of divine presence or interposition.[5] The same Hebrew word is used in Exodus 4:8–9, 30 with reference to the miraculous signs in Israel's deliverance from Egypt. Gideon wanted miraculous evidence that would leave no doubt that Israel's God had truly called him (6:17). Gideon may not

---

[5] Brown, Driver, and Briggs, *Hebrew and English Lexicon*, p. 16.

have been certain concerning the identity of his visitor, and Gideon's offering may indicate his determination to discover the identity of that one (6:18). Minhah, the Hebrew word translated "offering," may simply denote a gift or present (Gen. 32:13, 18; 43:11), tribute to a king (2 Kings 17:3–4), or offerings to God (Lev. 7:37; 23:37).[6] Keil and Delitzsch explain:

> Minchah does not mean a sacrifice in the strict sense ... but a sacrificial gift in the sense of a gift presented to God, on the acceptance of which he hoped to receive the sign, which would show whether the person who had appeared to him was really God. This sacrificial gift consisted of such food as they were accustomed to set before a guest whom they wished especially to honour.[7]

c) *Maturation of Gideon* (6:19–24)

The significance of Gideon's offering must be seen in relation to the scarcity of food at that time. The lengthy process of beating out the grain in the wine press would have yielded small results; yet Gideon took approximately forty pounds of flour, prepared a goat, and brought it to the angelic messenger. The angel of God instructed Gideon to place the offering on a rock that became an improvised altar (6:20). When the angel touched the offering with the tip of his staff, fire flared from the rock and consumed the meat and bread. This was a normal means by which the Lord indicated acceptance of an offering (Lev. 9:24; 1 Kings 18:38). Gideon had asked for and received a sign!

When Gideon recognized that the messenger had been the angel of the Lord, he was alarmed and thought he would die, for the Lord had previously told Moses, "No one may see me and live" (Exod. 33:20; cf. 20:19; Judg. 13:22; Isa. 6:5). The angel reassured Gideon that he would not die, whereupon Gideon constructed an altar to the Lord and named it "The LORD is Peace" (6:24). God had manifested Himself as a God of peace, and Gideon would worship God in the light of that manifestation. The altar served as a memorial to God to the very day the Book of Judges was written.

2. *Preparation of Gideon* (6:25–40)

a) *Destruction of idolatry* (6:25–33)

1) *Conquest of Gideon* (6:25–27). Gideon lived amid a syncretistic worship system in which the people attempted to worship both Baal and the Lord. If Gideon was going to serve the Lord, he would need

---

[6]Brown, Driver, and Briggs, *Hebrew and English Lexicon*, p. 585.
[7]Keil and Delitzsch, *Joshua, Judges, Ruth*, p. 333.

to indicate his disassociation from idolatry and his commitment to the Lord. Thus the Lord instructed Gideon to use his father's seven-year-old bull[8] to tear down the altar to Baal. By this initial act Gideon would display his loyalty to the Lord. The use of the bull in the demolition of the altar is significant. Cundall and Morris state that

> the bull was the sacred animal of the fertility cults. El himself, the head of the Canaanite pantheon, was often distinquished by the epithet "Bull." This particular animal may already have been designated for sacrifice to Baal.[9]

In addition to destroying the altar, Gideon was commanded to cut down the wooden pole that symbolized Asherah, the consort of Baal. Next, Gideon was told to construct an altar to the Lord (6:26) and offer a burnt offering on it, demonstrating his dedication to the Lord (Lev. 1:1-17). That this was a judgment on the Canaanite deity is clear from the following three considerations: (1) The sacred Canaanite bull was used to destroy the altar of Baal; (2) the Canaanite bull was sacrificed to the Lord; and (3) the Asherah was used as firewood for the offering!

Fearing opposition by Israelites who were sympathetic to Baalism, Gideon carried out the Lord's command at night with ten men assisting him.

2) *Contention of the Israelites* (6:28-33). The following morning the men of the city discovered the destoyed Canaanite altar and the newly constructed altar to the Lord. The dismantling of the Baal altar was no small chore:

> A Baal altar was found at Megiddo which measured some twenty-six feet across and four and a half feet high. Made of many stones, cemented together by mud, such an altar would constitute an immense task to destroy and carry away.[10]

When it became known that Gideon was responsible, the Baal worshipers came to Gideon's home and demanded that he be put to death for destroying the altar (6:30). Joash, Gideon's father, defended his son's action and threatened death to anyone who would oppose him. Thus it is clear that Joash had some authority, for he was able to influence the people. There was irony in Joash's statement in 6:31: "Are you going to plead Baal's cause? ... If Baal really is a god, he can defend himself when someone breaks down his altar." The irony is

---

[8]There is a textual problem of whether this is a reference to one or two bulls. Many (such as the NIV) understand this as referring to only one animal.

[9]Cundall and Morris, *Judges and Ruth*, p. 107.

[10]Wood, *Distressing Days*, p. 231.

reminiscent of Elijah's mocking statements to the Baal worshipers of his day (1 Kings 18:27).

As a result Joash renamed his son "Jerub-Baal" meaning, "let Baal contend" (6:32).

> This surname very soon became an honourable title for Gideon. When, for example, it became apparent to the people that Baal could not do him any harm, Jerubbaal became a Baal-fighter, one who had fought against Baal.[11]

Once more the Midianites invaded Israel on their annual foray into the land. They crossed the Jordan and camped in the Valley of Jezreel, the fertile area that extends completely across the land from the Jordan River to Mount Carmel on the Mediterranean Sea. As the only natural east-west valley that extends through the land, the terrain served as a convenient location for raids into the surrounding areas.[12]

b) *Descent of the Holy Spirit* (6:34–35)

In preparation for Gideon's great task of delivering Israel from oppression, the Spirit of the Lord came upon him. The phrase "came upon" literally means "clothed, i.e. took possession of him."[13] "The idea seems to be that the Spirit of the Lord incarnated Himself in Gideon and thus empowered him from within."[14] Now Gideon became a valiant warrior (6:12)! Endowed with the Spirit's power he blew the trumpet to summon the people to battle. The Abiezrites, his family clan (Josh. 17:2), were the first to respond. He also summoned the northern tribes of Asher, Zebulun and Naphtali who came out to meet the tribe of Manasseh in preparation for battle.

c) *Display of the fleece* (6:36–40)

1) *Dew on the fleece* (6:36–38). The timidity of Gideon became evident once more as he asked the Lord for a sign to assure him that God had truly chosen him as the vehicle through whom He would deliver Israel. He requested that when he would put a clipping of sheep's wool on the threshing floor, the sign would be revealed the following morning. If the fleece would be wet but the threshing floor dry, then it would be evident that the Lord had called him. The Lord granted his request; the following morning Gideon squeezed a bowlful of water from the fleece (6:38).

It should be pointed out that Gideon was employing the fleece as a

---

[11]Keil and Delitzsh, *Joshua, Judges, Ruth*, pp. 337–38.
[12]Cundall and Morris, *Judges and Ruth*, p. 108.
[13]Brown, Driver, and Briggs, *Hebrew and English Lexicon*, p. 528.
[14]Unger and White, *Nelson's Expository Dictionary*, p. 62.

sign to confirm God's will, not to discover it, for he already knew what God wanted him to do (6:14). The Lord had already told him to deliver Israel from Midian's oppression—that was God's will for him. It was weakness in Gideon's faith that demanded a sign; in fact, this was a second sign, for God had already given Gideon a sign that He would work through him (6:17, 21). A request for a sign is frequently seen in Scripture as either weakness of faith or unbelief (cf. Matt. 12:38; 1 Cor. 1:22–23).

2) *Dew on the ground* (6:39–40). To bolster his weak faith Gideon asked for a third sign in which he requested a reversal of the process. It would be a greater miracle to find the fleece dry and the threshing floor wet since the dew would naturally cling to the fleece. Moreover, Gideon recognized he was verging on putting God to the test (cf. Exod. 17:2, 7; Deut. 6:16; Ps. 95:9). Once more the Lord acceded to the request of Gideon—in the morning the dew was on the ground but the fleece was dry. God had confirmed that He would deliver Israel through Gideon.

3. *Conquests of Gideon* (7:1–8:21)

a) *Selection of troops* (7:1–8)

1) *Elimination of the fearful* (7:1–3). Having received the confirmation of victory from the Lord, Gideon led his men to the spring of Harod in the Valley of Jezreel, at the northern foot of Mount Gilboa. The Midianites, meanwhile, were camped only four miles away on the north side of the hill of Moreh.

As the preparations for battle were made, Gideon marshaled an army of thirty-two thousand men against the Midianites. Should the Israelites win the battle, they would take credit for the victory because of the strength of their numbers; hence, the Lord ordered a reduction. The important lesson that Gideon and his men were to learn was that numbers do not guarantee success. There possibly was a second reason for the reduction that is not directly mentioned in the text, but which is suggested in Deuteronomy 20:8. This verse specifies that a man was exempt from military service if he was fearful, lest he dishearten the other warriors. In any case after Gideon exempted the fearful, twenty-two thousand men went home and Gideon was left with ten thousand. His army was now outnumbered at more than thirteen to one!

The reference to Mount Gilead (7:3) is not clear since Gilead was east of the Jordan. It may be a reference to Gilboa.

2) *Elimination of the careless* (7:4–8). For God's purpose there were still too many soldiers. God informed Gideon that He would test the remaining ten thousand to determine which ones would go to war against the Midianites. While the first test eliminated the fearful, the second test was designed to eliminate the careless.

Gideon was instructed to separate those who knelt to drink from those that "lap the water with their tongues like a dog" (7:5). The test seems to be between those who knelt to drink and those who stood upright and lapped water with their hands. The men that knelt were careless and insensitive to possible attack and could have been surprised and overpowered by the enemy; the three hundred who remained standing showed that they were constantly alert. They could move into action more swiftly than those who had taken the time to kneel. The three hundred put defense and safety ahead of their personal comfort in getting sufficient water to drink. Ninety-seven hundred soldiers got their pink slips!

The phrase "lap the water with their tongues like a dog" (7:5) is explained by the succeeding phrase, "lapped with their hands to their mouths" (v. 6). "The 300 used their hands as a dog uses its tongue to scoop up the water while they remained on their feet, watchful and prepared for any emergency."[15]

b) *Preparation for battle* (7:9–18)

1) *Investigation of the Midianite camp* (7:9–14). The Lord's command to Gideon was immediate: "Get up, go down against the camp, because I am going to give it into your hands" (7:9). Yet Gideon was afraid; so God allowed him to gain further assurance. The Lord commanded Gideon to take Purah, his servant, and steal into the Midianite camp to discover the distraught spirit in the enemy ranks (7:9–10). Purah was Gideon's attendant or armorbearer (Heb. *na'ar*; cf. 9:54; 16:26; 1 Sam. 14:1, 6).[16] After hearing what the people in the camp had to say, Gideon would be encouraged to attack the Midianites with his three hundred men.

Gideon and Purah approached the outposts of the camp, for this was where they would be attacking (cf. 7:17, 19). Before them the Midianites and Amalekites seemed to fill the valley as thick as locusts (7:12). The hyperbole is very apt, for just as the locusts devasted and de-

---

[15]Cundall and Morris, *Judges and Ruth*, p. 110.
[16]Brown, Driver, and Briggs, *Hebrew and English Lexicon*, pp. 654–55; cf. Unger and White, *Nelson's Expository Dictionary*, pp. 487–88.

voured the land, so the intruders had plundered and stripped the land. Gideon's three hundred troops were sorely outnumbered by the 135,000 enemy soldiers that lay before them (8:10). As Gideon and Purah listened, they overheard one sentry relating his dream to a friend. Dreams had great significance in Eastern culture, and the Old Testament portrays God as revealing future events through dreams on various occasions (cf. Gen 37:5–11; 40:5–22; Dan. 2:1–45; 4:4–28; 7:1–28).

The sentry told of seeing a loaf of barley bread tumbling into the camp with such force that when it struck a tent the tent collapsed (7:13). The interpretation of the dream is given in verse 14. The barley bread was the staple of the poor people and here denoted Israel in poverty because of Midianite oppression. Specifically, it represented Gideon with his three hundred men invading the Midianite camp. The tent signified the nomadic home of the Midianites, while the collapsed tent indicated the conquest of the Midianites by Gideon. As Gideon overheard the second sentry give the interpretation of the dream, he received his final assurance concerning Israel's conquest. God had given Gideon a fourth sign—surely an indication of God's patience in dealing with the fearful and unbelieving!

2) *Organization into companies* (7:15–18). Having heard the prophecy of Israel's victory from the mouths of the Midianites, Gideon worshiped the Lord. His faith was bolstered and he returned to camp with words similar to the Lord's (cf. 7:9, 15). He divided the three hundred men into three companies, a common feature in Old Testament warfare (1 Sam. 11:11; 2 Sam. 18:2). The men were all given trumpets and empty jars with torches inside the jars and instructed to follow the example of Gideon. The jars were important to concealing the torches until the latter were ready for use. The trumpet was a ram's horn (Hebrew, *shopar*)[17] and was used to summon the troops to battle (3:27; 2 Sam. 20:1). Cundall is no doubt correct when he suggests the Israelites intended to make as much noise as possible; hence, the trumpets would not have been blown only once but the Israelites would have continued blowing them. He suggests the sequence was a blast of the trumpets, the crash of the pitchers, and the battle cry "For the LORD and for Gideon," followed by further trumpet blasts. As the Israelites

---

[17]For a helpful brief discussion see Hermann J. Austel, "שֹׁפָר," *Theological Wordbook of the Old Testament*, R. Laird Harris, Gleason L. Archer, Jr., and Bruce K. Waltke, eds., vol. 2 (Chicago: Moody Press, 1980), pp. 951–52.

pursued the Midianites, they would have alternated between shouts and blasts from the trumpets.[18] The purpose of the Israelites was both to confuse the Midianites and to convince them that they were surrounded by an innumerable host.

c) *Destruction of Midian* (7:19–25)

1) *Surprise attack* (7:19–23). At the beginning of the middle watch Gideon and his men attacked. The night was divided into three watches of four hours each, beginning at 6:00 P.M.; hence, the middle watch began at 10:00 P.M. The attack was well planned as Cundall suggests:

> Those not involved in the first or second watches would be in the deep sleep of the earlier part of the night, whilst those who had just been relieved would still be moving about the camp, thus increasing the fear of those awakened by the din, that the enemy had already penetrated the camp.[19]

It is possible, as Cundall indicates, that a camel stampede added to the confusion.

Gideon and his men surrounded the Midianite camp. As Gideon gave the signal, all three hundred men blew their trumpets, smashed their jars, held the torches aloft, and shouted, "A sword for the LORD and for Gideon!" (7:20). In the confusion the people in the camp leaped up, cried out, and fled, thinking they were surrounded by a large army. Gideon's followers stood in position surrounding the camp with their torches, thus giving the appearance of a multitude of soldiers. In the confusion the Midianites began to kill one another (v. 22). Finally, the Midianites fled eastward down the valley toward the Jordan from where they had originally invaded Israel. To complete the rout, Gideon summoned Israelites from the tribes of Naphtali, Asher, and Manasseh to pursue the fleeing Midianites (v. 23).

2) *Unified attack* (7:24–25). As the Midianites fled southward, Gideon summoned additional help from the Ephraimites to guard the fords of the Jordan, preventing the Midianites from escaping across the river. The location of Beth Barah ("town of fords") is unknown, but it may have been near Wadi Far'ah. The Ephraimites captured and killed the two Midianite leaders, Oreb ("raven") and Zeeb ("wolf"). The locations of the victories, rock of Oreb and wine press of Zeeb, are unknown; the names were given where the two Midianite leaders were

---

[18]Cundall and Morris, *Judges and Ruth*, p. 113.
[19]Cundall and Morris, *Judges and Ruth*, p. 113.

killed. The heads of the two leaders were brought to Gideon as trophies of the victory, a common custom in the East (1 Sam. 17:51; 31:8–9).

d) *Placation of Ephraim* (8:1–3)

Although a great victory had been achieved, there was tribal jealousy. Ephraim was angered that Gideon had not asked them earlier to join the battle (probably a reference to Gideon's initial summons in 6:35). It is possible that Ephraim's anger was aroused because they did not receive a share in the spoils of the battle. Gideon's response is noteworthy and reminiscent of Proverbs 15:1: "A gentle answer turns away wrath." In his response in 8:2 Gideon used a proverbial statement to depreciate his own part in the victory and to compliment Ephraim on their achievement. The phrase "the gleanings of Ephraim's grapes" refers to Ephraim killing the two Midianite leaders, while the phrase "the full grape harvest of Abiezer" refers to the victory by the three hundred men and Gideon. As a result of Gideon's soft reply the Ephraimites were assuaged. The Hebrew word for "resentment" is *ruah*, the normal word for "wind" or "spirit." The connotation of breath has a wide variety of meanings, among them, "courage" (Josh. 2:11; 5:1), being "overwhelmed" (1 Kings 10:5), or "resentment" or "anger," as a rush of air, a snort through one's nose (Judg. 8:3; Prov. 29:11).[20]

e) *Retribution of Succoth and Peniel* (8:4–21)

1) *Mockery* (8:4–9). Gideon not only defeated the Midianites but he also pursued the remaining Midianites, hoping thereby to completely rid Israel of their menacing raids. He took only the three hundred men in the pursuit and continued the chase even though his tiny army was exhausted. When they came to Succoth, a town lying just north of the Jabbok River and east of the Jordan, Gideon requested food for his troops. The sarcastic response of the officials shows a repudiation for Gideon and his venture, as well as a proud refusal to give any aid to assist their fellow Israelites in capturing a common enemy. If not dealt with, such an attitude would foster disunity in the nation, for the response ridiculed the possibility of Gideon and his tired men capturing Zebah and Zalmunna: "Do you already have the hands of Zebah and Zalmunna in your possession?" (8:6).

The harsh response of Gideon stands in marked contrast to his re-

---

[20]J. Barton Payne, "רִיחַ," *Theological Wordbook*, vol. 2, pp. 836–37; Robert B. Girdlestone, *Synonyms of the Old Testament* (Grand Rapids: Eerdmans, 1974 reprint), p. 60.

sponse to the Ephraimites (cf. 8:2–3, 7) and reveals the disloyalty and treason of the people of Succoth. Gideon warned that he would tear their flesh with desert thorns and briers. This may refer to dragging their bodies over sharp thorns and briers, or it may mean threshing sledges shod with sharp stones or metal points would be pulled over their bodies.[21] The punishment was certain to end in death.

When Gideon and his men came to Peniel, which was east of Succoth, the response was similar (8:8). As a result Gideon also pronounced a judgment on that city, promising to tear down its tower, the stronghold of the town.

2) *Mission* (8:10–12). In their flight, Zebah and Zalmunna had come to Karkor near the Wadi Sirhan to the east of the Dead Sea.

> The wells of Karkar or Keraker are situated in a capacious basin surrounded by almost impassable limestone hills, from which only a single convenient but not very broad outlet leads to the depression of Sirhan. The suggestion is that Gideon, having stationed some of his men at this opening, might with others climb the hills surrounding the basin, and so take the camp by surprise.[22]

The devastation by Gideon is seen in that only fifteen thousand men remained of the Midianite army; one hundred and twenty thousand swordsmen had already fallen (8:10).

In his pursuit of the remaining Midianites, Gideon followed the caravan route southeastward ("the route of the nomads")[23] past Nobah and Jogbehah. The former is unknown and the latter was fifteen miles southeast of Peniel. In a surprise attack against the Midianite army, Gideon captured their two kings.

3) *Misery* (8:13–21). Having captured the kings, Gideon returned to Succoth by the Pass of Heres (the location is unknown today). Gideon captured a youth from Succoth and obtained the names of seventy-seven officials of the town, the men responsible for refusing to give help to Gideon and his men.

> This is the first mention of a town's elders in the book. They make up the corporate governing body where there is no one called king. Some of them will also be "commanders" or past commanders, the number seventy-seven standing for the total of adult free males who are heads of families.[24]

[21]Gray, *Joshua, Judges and Ruth*, pp. 309–10; Cundall and Morris, *Judges and Ruth*, p. 116.

[22]Garstang, *Joshua-Judges*, p. 323, see map p. 322, and description p. 390.

[23]Aharoni, *Land of the Bible*, p. 241.

[24]Boling, *Judges*, AB, p. 157.

The young man wrote down the names of the seventy-seven officials. The earliest known writing is Sumerian and antedates 3000 B.C.[25] The youth probably inscribed the names of the officials on potsherds.

With the two Midianite kings as evidence of his conquest, Gideon returned to Succoth and reminded them of their taunt. Then he fulfilled his threat by disciplining the men of Succoth and tearing down the tower of Peniel and killing the men (8:16–17).

> The punishment inflicted by Gideon upon both the cities was well deserved in all respects, and was righteously executed. The inhabitants of these cities had not only acted treacherously to Israel as far as they could, from the most selfish interests, in a holy conflict for the glory of the Lord and the freedom of His people, but in their contemptuous treatment of Gideon and his host they had poured contempt upon the Lord.[26]

On questioning Zebah and Zalmunna, Gideon discovered that the kings apparently had murdered his brothers at home and not in battle. The brothers of Gideon were identifiable by their princely stature and bearing (cf. 1 Sam. 9:2; 16:7, 18). Had the kings not killed his brothers, Gideon would have spared their lives; however, they brought the law of revenge by the kinsman-redeemer on themselves (Deut. 19:12). Gideon was going to add insult to injury by having his son, Jether, slay the kings—it would have been an honor for the eldest son, but a decided insult for the kings. However, Jether was afraid since he was just a boy. In stoical fashion the kings called on Gideon, himself, to do the job; thus they would escape the indignity of dying at the hands of a boy and die honorably at the hands of a great warrior. "So Gideon stepped forward and killed them, and took the ornaments off their camels' necks" (8:21). The moon-shaped ornaments were probably used as amulets to ward off evil spirits.

4. Conclusion of Gideon (8:22–27)

a) Evil request of Israel (8:22–23)

Following Gideon's great victory over the Midianites, the Israelites invited Gideon to establish a dynastic rule over the nation. It is uncertain how many tribes were involved in the request—perhaps only the northern tribes that were primarily involved in the Midianite oppression. It was an evil request, for Israel was a theocracy under the direct

---

[25]For a very helpful article with an extensive bibliography, see W. White, Jr., "Writing," ZPEB, 5:995–1015.
[26]Keil and Delitzsch, *Joshua, Judges, Ruth*, p. 354.

rule of God. Their relationship as subjects to the Lord their King was established in Exodus 19. Their petition to Gideon was in essence a rejection of the Lord as their King; moreover, it expressed their desire to have a king rule over them like other nations (cf. 1 Sam. 8:5ff.; 10:19). Gideon rejected their invitation to establish a monarchy; however, Israel's request anticipated the rule of Abimelech (9:1–57) and the institution of the monarchy under Saul (1 Sam. 8).

b) *Evil practice of Israel* (8:24–27)

This section is anticlimactic in relation to the great achievements of Gideon. Although the motive for Gideon's action is uncertain, he was responsible for leading the nation into idolatry. Since the ephod was closely associated with discerning the will of the Lord (Exod. 28:6–30), it is possible that Gideon attempted to provide a mechanical means whereby the people could discover God's will. However, his action was a sin and a tragic error.

Gideon collected the gold earrings the people had obtained from the Ishmaelites. The term Ishmaelites is used as a synonym here for Midianites (cf. Gen. 37:28) although the Ishmaelites were descendants of Abraham through Hagar (Gen. 16:16), while the Midianites descended through Keturah (Gen. 25:1–2). The accumulation of gold earrings came to seventeen hundred shekels, about forty-two pounds. From the gold Gideon made an ephod, a garment usually worn by the high priest of Israel. Attached to the high priest's ephod was the Urim and Thummim, which were used to discern the Lord's will (Exod. 28:30; cf. 1 Sam. 23:9–12). Probably Gideon's ephod, or vest, was different from that of the Israelite high priest since Gideon's garment would have been too heavy to wear.

Gideon installed the ephod at Ophrah, and "all Israel prostituted themselves by worshiping it" (8:27). The Hebrew term for "prostituted themselves" literally means to "commit fornication; be a harlot," and is used of physical prostitution (Gen. 38:24); in this instance the term conveys "intercourse with other deities," which was considered spiritual prostitution and sometimes also involved immoral physical acts.[27]

Gideon's sin was twofold: (1) he usurped the function of the priest, which was wrong for him since he was not a Levite; and (2) he established a worship center in the wrong place—at Ophrah—instead of worshiping at Shiloh.[28]

---

[27]Brown, Driver, and Briggs, *Hebrew and English Lexicon*, pp. 275–76.
[28]Wood, *Distressing Days*, p. 227.

5. *Silence: forty years* (8:28–32)

The victory over the Midianites brought peace to the land for forty years—one generation.

The verses that conclude Gideon's biography, not only record the tragic conclusion to his life, but also serve as an introduction for the events to follow with his son Abimelech. The chaotic condition of the period is further seen in the polygamy of Gideon, who had seventy sons from his many wives (8:30). Gideon had a concubine in Shechem —the statement probably suggests a matralineal marriage in which the wife remained in her parental home. Out of this union was born Abimelech ("father of a king"), a cognomen given to him later in life to depict his character—he expected to be the father of a king.[29]

For Further Study

1. Study life of Gideon, noting his strengths and weaknesses.

2. What is the difference, if any, between humility and inferiority or weakness?

3. Develop a concordance study of "God's will" and the "will of God," noting the specific areas in which the will of God is revealed (for example, 1 Thess. 4:3; 5:18).

4. Was Gideon justified in taking action against Succoth and Peniel? When is it justifiable for us to take the law into our own hands?

---

[29]Keil and Delitzsch, *Joshua, Judges, Ruth*, p. 360.

Chapter 6

Fifth Cycle of Oppression
(Judges 8:33–10:5)

The increased depravity of the nation Israel is seen in the accession of the renegade king, Abimelech. The people of Shechem and surrounding area came under the bondage of Abimelech, the son of Gideon by a Canaanite woman of Shechem. Abimelech ruled three years (9:22) and then sustained the judgment of God when a woman killed him (9:50–57).

A. Sin: idolatry (8:33–9:6)

1. *Idolatry of Israel* (8:33–35)

The Israelites whom Gideon had delivered apostatized immediately on his death, revealing their spiritual weakness and inability to stand firm unless they had a strong leader. It was characteristic that when a judge died in Israel, the people apostatized.

Israel's continuing sin of Baal worship intensified following Gideon's death when "they set up Baal-Berith as their god" (8:33). The name Baal-Berith ("Lord of the covenant") is virtuously synonymous with El-Berith ("God of the covenant," 9:46). This may mean that several Canaanite cities united in a league of common interest for the purpose of worshiping Baal at a central shrine, which in this instance was at Shechem (9:46). The Israelites in Abimelech's area joined this league of Canaanite cities in the worship of Baal, forgetting the Lord God to whom they had been covenanted at Sinai (Exod. 19). Not only did they forget the Lord, but they also forgot Gideon, the Baal-fighter who had delivered them from the Midianites. Thus their repentance was short-lived.

2. *Depravity of Abimelech* (9:1–6)

Abimelech's aspiration to become king was put into motion when he visited his mother's clan in Shechem. It appears Abimelech was never integrated into the social life of his father's family, which may be the ultimate reason for his murderous action against his stepbrothers (9:5).

Abimelech approached the inhabitants of Shechem and aroused them against his seventy brothers, referring to them as "sons of Jerub-Baal," that is, "sons of Baal-fighters," suggesting Gideon's seventy sons were as ready to eradicate Baal worship in Israel as Gideon. Moreover, Abimelech suggested that Gideon's seventy sons aspired to rule over the people although there is nothing to indicate this was true. Abimelech gave two reasons as to why he should be acknowledged as king: 1) one ruler would be better than seventy; 2) he was related by blood to the people of Shechem (cf. 8:31). When the brothers of Abimelech's mother spoke to the inhabitants of Shechem on Abimelech's behalf, the populace indicated their approval of him (9:3).

To illustrate their support of Abimelech, the people of Shechem gave him seventy silver shekels from the temple of Baal-Berith. The seventy shekels represented one for each of the seventy sons of Gideon. With the money Abimelech hired "reckless adventurers, who became his followers" (9:4). The designation "reckless" (Hebrew, *rek*) literally means empty, thus idle or worthless ethically.[1] The emptiness would refer to the men being devoid of wisdom or moral understanding (cf. 11:3; 2 Chron. 13:7).

The desire of Abimelech to be king led to tragic results as he "went to his father's home in Ophrah and on one stone murdered his seventy brothers" (9:5). The account does not describe a battle but rather a ritualistic execution. The reference to "one stone" denotes a stone for sacrificing animals; the stone was the customary place for sacrificial slaughter (1 Sam. 14:33). Moore notes that

> the very conformity to the precautions taken in slaughtering animals in the open field shows that the motive was to dispose of the blood, in which was the life of his victims, in such a way that they should give him no further trouble.[2]

Of the seventy sons of Gideon only Jotham, the youngest, escaped the carnage.

Being in agreement the citizens of Shechem and Beth Millo crowned

---

[1]Brown, Driver, and Briggs, *Hebrew and English Lexicon*, p. 938.
[2]Moore, "Judges," ICC, pp. 242–43.

Abimelech king (9:6). Beth Millo literally means "house of the fortress" and is probably synonymous with the "tower of Shechem" in verse 46.

> Millo is a common noun, the Akkadian cognate of which denotes an artificial earthwork, terrace, or embankment. At Jerusalem it may denote the "filling out" by terrace and buttress of the steep slope and particularly the depression to the east between the ancient settlement on the south-east hill and the north-east, or Temple, hill in Solomon's time. Wright has established that the temple (probably that of El-berith) and its precinct stood on an artificial "fill", or esplanade which is denoted by *millo*. Thus the people of Shechem and of Beth-millo may denote not two distinct settlements but rather the people of the settlement in general and an upper stratum, perhaps descended from the class of professional soldiers so characteristic of the city-states of Syro-Palestine in the Amarna Age (15th–14th centuries.).[3]

B. Servitude: Abimelech (9:7–57)

1. *Parable of Jotham* (9:7–15)

When Jotham heard that Abimelech had been installed as king by the Shechemites, he climbed up Mount Gerizim and shouted to the people. Mount Gerizim was significant in Israel's history, for there the blessings of the Mosaic Law had been proclaimed to the people on their entrance into the land (cf. Deut. 11:29; 27:12; Josh. 8:33). Now from the same location Jotham denounced the folly of the Shechemites. With Mount Gerizim and Mount Ebal rising on either side of Shechem, a natural amphitheater was created. In all probability Jotham did not ascend to the top of Gerizim but chose a natural ledge above the town; thus the townspeople could hear him, and he could escape should they pursue him.

Jotham told a parable concerning the action of the Shechemites in crowning Abimelech as their king. In the parable the trees wanted someone to reign over them and approached the olive tree first, inviting it to reign over the rest of the trees (9:8). The olive tree was useful in several ways: its fruit was a staple for food, its oil was used to anoint priests and kings and was also soothing for the skin, and its wood served as fuel. There could be no doubt that the olive tree was very useful. But the olive tree refused to reign since it had an important place of service to gods ("God," NASB) and men. Then the other trees approached the fig tree, asking it to reign over them (v. 10), but this tree also refused. It declined to leave its fruit, so "good and sweet," and

---

[3]Gray, *Joshua, Judges and Ruth*, CB, pp. 317–18; see also G. Ernest Wright, *Shechem* (New York: McGraw-Hill Co., 1965), pp. 80ff.

go reign over the other trees (v. 11). Many varieties of figs exist and they were a delicious and important staple for the nation, sometimes being dried and pressed into cakes (1 Sam. 25:18). When the fig tree also refused to reign, the trees approached the vine, saying, "Come and be our king" (9:12). The vine also refused, saying, "Should I give up my wine, which cheers both gods (*Elohim* may be translated either "gods" or "God," as in the NASB) and men?" (9:13). The product of the vine was useful to both God and men, the wine being used as a libation offering to God (Num. 15:7; 28:7) and as the common drink for the people.

When the vine also refused, the trees approached the thornbush, saying, "Come and be our king" (9:14). The thornbush accepted the invitation, inviting the trees to take refuge in its shade. The offer of protection from the sun was meaningless since the thornbush casts virtually no shadow. With the acceptance came a warning toward those who would not support the thornbush: "then let fire come out of the thornbush and consume the cedars of Lebanon!" (9:15). The dry thornbush was a common source of starting and spreading fires (Exod. 22:6; Isa. 9:18); hence, the threat was not an empty one. The uselessness and danger of the thornbush were well known:

> (It) not only produced nothing of value and was quite worthless as timber, but was a positive menace to the farmer who had to wage continual war against its encroachments. Its carpet-like growth was an especial menace in the heat of summer when scrub fires, fanned by the wind, could travel at incredible speeds along the tinder of dried brambles.[4]

The interpretation of the parable was clear: the trees represented the people of Shechem; the olive, fig, and vine represented Gideon (cf. 9:16ff.), and the thornbush represented Abimelech—a worthless king who would prove a menace to them.

2. Denunciation of Jotham (9:16–21)

Jotham applied the parable in his denunciation of the people of Shechem. In his rebuke Jotham reminded them of Gideon's faithful service in risking his life to rescue them from the Midianites. In the parenthetical statement in 9:17–18 Jotham reminded them of their revolt against Gideon's family; he spoke too of their guilt in the death of Gideon's seventy sons by association with Abimelech and by providing him with money from their temple (v. 4). Jotham ridiculed their

---

[4]Cundall and Morris, *Judges and Ruth*, p. 129.

choice: they had rejected the brave warrior Gideon and had instead chosen the worthless son of a slave girl as their king! In verse 19 Jotham resumed the thought begun in verse 16. If they had acted in honesty and good faith, he wished them well! If their choice had been dishonorable, might they experience disunity and discord! Jotham's words had the ring of prophecy since his prediction of disharmony was soon fulfilled (vv. 22–25).

While the response of the people of Shechem is not given, it appears they pursued Jotham, who fled to Beer ("well") following his denunciation (9:21). The site of the town of Beer has not been identified.

3. *Dispute of Shechem* (9:22–25)

After Abimelech had ruled "Israel" for three years, the prediction of Jotham came to pass with disharmony developing between the people of Shechem and Abimelech. God punished both Abimelech and the Shechemites by sending an evil spirit between them (cf. 1 Sam. 16:14–15).[5] "'An evil spirit' is not merely 'an evil disposition,' but an evil demon, which produced discord and strife, just as an evil spirit came upon Saul."[6]

The purpose of God's judgment, as explicitly stated in 9:24, was to avenge the death of the seventy sons of Gideon by Abimelech and the people of Shechem. The spirit of dissension came to fruition when when the citizens of Shechem "set men on the hilltops to ambush and rob everyone who passed by" (v. 25). The hill country of Ephraim was ideal for this at Shechem.

> The most important latitudinal road ascends from the vicinity of Socoh in the Sharon to Samaria and Shechem. From here it joins the longitudinal road and goes north-east as far as Tirzah, whence it descends via the Wadi Far'ah to the important fords of the Jordan near the city of Adam. This is the most convenient line by which one may cross the central hill country and helps to explain the rise of important cities on the sites of Shechem and Tirzah, and later also Samaria, at major highway junctures.[7]

Although it is not stated, Abimelech possibly collected tolls from the

---

[5]It should be remembered that although God tests people or judges unbelievers, He never solicits them to sin (James 1:13). Furthermore, although God has decreed all things that come to pass, He is never responsible for sin. Berkhof makes an important distinction between God effecting the decree Himself and permitting the free expression of His creatures, generally called God's permissive decree; cf. L. Berkhof, *Systematic Theology* (Grand Rapids: Eerdmans, 1941), p. 103.

[6]Keil and Delitzsch, *Joshua, Judges, Ruth*, p. 365.

[7]Aharoni, *Land of the Bible*, pp. 55–56.

numerous travelers who passed Shechem. The men of Shechem ambushed these travelers, apparently depriving Abimelech of the tolls he would otherwise have collected. The narrator in concluding says that "this was reported to Abimelech" (9:25), indicating the warfare that would erupt as a result.

4. Defiance of Gaal (9:26–49)

Gaal, the son of Ebed, was an opportunist who moved one day with his brothers to Shechem. The inhabitants were looking for a new leader, having rejected Abimelech, and Gaal gained their trust. At the time of the grape harvest Gaal publicly repudiated Abimelech. The festival was the Shechemite counterpart to the Israelite Feast of Tabernacles.[8] Amid the wine drinking, shouting, and merrymaking, Gaal proudly boasted, "Who is Abimelech, and who is Shechem, that we should be subject to him?" (9:28). Gaal answered his own question, reminding the people of Abimelech's parentage. It is noteworthy that while Abimelech appealed to the people on the basis of his mother being a Shechemite (vv. 2–3), Gaal reminded the people that Jerub-Baal, the Baal-fighter, was his father (v. 28). This was a vivid reminder to the citizens of Shechem that Abimelech's father had destroyed Baal worship and installed the worship of the Lord. The question concerning Shechem is explained in the question "Isn't Zebul his deputy?" (v. 28), suggesting that it was unnecessary for the people to serve Zebul. Gaal exhorted the people of Shechem to reject Israelite rule and return to Canaanite rule (cf. "men of Hamor, Shechem's father"; Gen. 33:19). In offering himself to the people as their leader, Gaal challenged Abimelech to attack Shechem (9:29).

When Zebul, the governor of the city, heard the boastful words of Gaal, he became angry and informed Abimelech. It appears that Zebul was not actually a deputy of Abimelech; rather, the statement of 9:28 is to be understood as ridicule and scorn toward Zebul, who was a commandant,[9] or governor, of the city appointed by Abimelech to represent him.[10] However, because of the opposition of Gaal and his men, Zebul secretly sent messengers to Abimelech to inform him that Gaal was stirring up the city against him (v. 31). Along with the information Zebul sent a suggestion: they should "lie in wait" or set an ambush

---

[8]Bruce, "Judges," NBC, p. 266.
[9]Brown, Driver, and Briggs, *Hebrew and English Lexicon*, p. 978.
[10]Moore, *Judges*, p. 258.

against the city of Shechem (vv. 32–33). The Hebrew word *arab*, translated "lie in wait" here, is used forty times in the Old Testament, with fourteen occurrences in Judges and seven in Joshua. "In the majority of these twenty-one instances, ambush as a method of warfare is described."[11] The capture of Ai (Josh. 8) and the war against the Benjamites (Judg. 20) are described by this Hebrew term.

Taking Zebul's advice, Abimelech divided his men into four companies (cf. 7:16; 1 Sam. 11:11; 13:17) and lay in ambush for Gaal (9:34). Gaal came out of Shechem and stood at the city's entrance, completely unprepared when Abimelech and his men began their assault (v. 35). As he looked he saw the people approaching from the tops of the mountains—no doubt Ebal and Gerizim (v. 36). But Zebul scoffed at Gaal, purposely intending to deceive him so as to give Abimelech more time to advance (v. 36). Gaal was persistent: "Look, people are coming down from the center (literally, navel) of the land, and a company is coming from the direction of the soothsayers' tree" (v. 37). The center of the land may refer to an elevation possibly Gerizim, or where the narrow east-west pass empties into the broader north-south plain.[12] The reference to the soothsayers' tree may refer to the great tree of Moreh (cf. Gen. 12:6).

When Abimelech and his men came into view, Zebul no longer concealed his alignment; he reproached Gaal for his boasting, saying, "Where is your big talk (literally, 'your (big) mouth') now?" (9:38). Zebul's ridicule and Abimelech's confrontation forced Gaal into battle with Abimelech to avoid humiliation. As a result Gaal led an ill-prepared contingent of Shechemites against Abimelech (v. 39). The outcome was swift with Gaal being defeated and driven from Shechem and the wounded Shechemites littering the field all the way to the gate of the city (v. 40). Abimelech, however, did not take possession of Shechem but remained in Arumah, situated in the hills a short distance from Shechem.[13]

The next day Abimelech was notified (9:42) when the people of Shechem went out to the field to work in the vineyards (not on ambush raids as in v. 25). He gathered his men, divided them into three companies, and ambushed the Shechemites as they came out of the city. One company rushed to the entrance of the city, prohibiting any

---

[11]Victor P. Hamilton, "אָרַב," *Theological Wordbook*, vol. 1, p. 68.
[12]Cf. Gray, *Joshua, Judges and Ruth*, CB, p. 324; pp. 178–79.
[13]Boling, *Judges*, AB, see illustration 6.

retreat, while the other two companies massacred the Shechemites in the field (v. 44). The ambush was a retaliation against those who questioned Abimelech's leadership and for breaking a covenant with him. After killing the people Abimelech sowed the city with salt. It was a symbolic act, "signifying that the city was to be turned for ever into a barren salt desert. Salt ground is a barren desert (see Job xxxix. 6, Ps. cvii. 34)."[14]

When the people inside the city heard what Abimelech had done, they took refuge inside the stronghold of the temple of El-Berith (see at 9:6). Gray explains the stronghold:

> In Nabataean funerary inscriptions it denotes a rock-hewn tomb. This might suggest a crypt or a rock-hewn chamber over which the temple was built, perhaps the original sanctuary, and so a natural place of refuge when the men of the Tower of Shechem despaired of resistance.[15]

Inside the stronghold of the temple of El-Berith the people sought the help of their god. El-Berith is seen as synonymous with Baal-Berith (9:4; see comment at 8:33). The god El was replaced by Baal, the Canaanite fertility god.

In his final assault on Shechem, Abimelech gathered his men at Mount Zalmon ("shaded" or "dark"), possibly a reference to either Ebal or Gerizim with the heavily wooded forests. Since the temple stronghold had a wooden roof, Abimelech and his men cut down trees, placed them on the roof of the building, and set them on fire. About one thousand Shechemites died in the resulting conflagration. The prophetic words of Jotham were literally fulfilled (9:20).

5. *Death of Abimelech* (9:50–55)

Following the conquest of Shechem, Abimelech attacked Thebez, possibly Tubas, located thirteen miles north of Shechem; apparently Thebez had joined the revolt of Shechem against Abimelech. When Abimelech captured the city, the people fled into the fortress-temple as in Shechem. Abimelech was determined to destroy the stronghold by burning it just as he had successfully done at Shechem (9:52). But as Abimelech approached the tower, a woman dropped an upper millstone on his head and cracked his skull. The upper millstone, smaller than the lower millstone, was twelve to eighteen inches in diameter and serveral inches thick—certainly a formidable weapon! To

---

[14]Keil and Delitzsch, *Joshua, Judges, Ruth*, p. 370.
[15]Gray, *Joshua, Judges and Ruth*, CB, p. 325.

avoid the humiliation of having been killed by a woman, Abimelech quickly called for his armorbearer to kill him with a sword (cf. 8:21; 1 Sam. 31:4). When the Israelites who had supported Abimelech saw that he was dead, they went home (9:55). Although Abimelech had killed the seventy sons of Gideon, he nonetheless had the support of at least some Israelites in his war with the Shechemites, who represented a Canaanite rebellion.[16]

6. *Declaration* (9:56–57)

The outworking of God's judgment on Abimelech and the people of Shechem was now complete, for the curse of Jotham was fulfilled as Abimelech and the Shechemites met their death (cf. 9:20). The statement emphasizes that God judged both groups.

> The Hebrews overlooked what might be called secondary causes and saw in these events the direct action of *God*, the evidence of His sovereignty within history, in the judgment upon Abimelech and the fulfilment of the curse of Jotham upon the Shechemites.[17]

C. Salvation: Tola and Jair (10:1–2a, 3a, 4–5)

After recording the death of Abimelech the narrator mentions two minor judges. These were no doubt local individuals who did not judge all twelve of the tribes and probably did not perform any unusual feats since none are recalled.

The first of these minor judges was Tola, son of Puah, the son of Dodo. Little is known of Tola (probably meaning "worm"), who belonged to the tribe of Issachar. Tola and Puah are also names of the family clans of Issachar (Gen. 46:13; Num. 26:23; 1 Chron. 7:1). Tola's function as a judge is seen in the phrase "(he) rose to save Israel" (10:1), suggesting he delivered Israel from an oppressor; but the oppressor is not named. Tola was the grandson of Dodo ("his beloved") and lived at Shamir in the hill country of Ephraim. The site of Shamir (not the town of Judah mentioned in Joshua 15:48) is unknown.

After the death of Tola another minor judge, Jair of Gilead, rose up in Israel. Jair ("he enlightens") was a wealthy, prominent man from the tribe of Manasseh (Num. 32:41). The statement "He had thirty sons, who rode thirty donkeys" (10:4) suggests the harem, prestige, and wealth of Jair. In the days when Israel had no horses, donkeys were

---

[16]Moore, *Judges*, pp. 268–69.
[17]Cundall and Morris, *Judges and Ruth*, p. 136.

considered a mark of distinction (cf. 1:14; 5:10; 12:14; 1 Sam. 25:20). The thirty towns were tent-villages[18] (cf. Deut. 3:14; Josh. 13:30; 1 Kings 4:13) and were called Havvoth Jair ("the tent-villages of Jair"). This designation, given earlier to an ancestor named Jair (Num. 32:41), again came into prominence during the days of the Jair of the Book of Judges. At Jair's death he was buried at Kamon in the territory of Manasseh southeast of the Sea of Galilee.

D. Silence: forty-five years (10:2b, 3b)

The combined judgeships of Tola and Jair totaled forty-five years.

For Further Study

1. Study the transition from Gideon to Abimelech and discuss this question: how does one sin affect another?

2. What are the negative lessons or warnings to learn from the life of Abimelech?

3. Read an article on parables in a Bible dictionary or encyclopedia, noting particularly the use of parables in the Old Testament.

4. Study the concept of deception by different people in the story of Abimelech; then notice the biblical emphasis through a concordance study of the word deceit.

---

[18]Brown, Driver, and Briggs, *Hebrew and English Lexicon*, p. 295.

Chapter 7

Sixth Cycle of Oppression
(Judges 10:6-12:15)

In the development of the period of the Judges, two major emphases are observable in this chapter: (1) the increasing intensity of Israel's sin and depravity, emphasized in the detailed enumeration of their idolatry (10:6); (2) the Lord's severe chastisement of His straying people through two major oppressors, the Philistines and the Ammonites (v. 7).

A. Sin: idolatry (10:6)

The sin of Israel intensified as the people fell deeper into idolatry. The narrator emphasized the increased moral lapse by his deliberate enumeration of the foreign deities that the Israelites served. It is noteworthy that seven categories of false deities are mentioned in 10:6, while in verses 11-12, the narrator lists seven foreign nations from whom the Lord delivered Israel. Keil and Delitzsch say that

> the correspondence between the number seven in these two cases and the significant use of the number are unmistakeable. Israel had balanced the number of divine deliverances by a similar number of idols which it served, so that the measure of the nation's iniquity was filled up in the same proportion as the measure of the delivering grace of God.[1]

Once more Israel served the Baals and the Ashtoreths—the plural form denoting all false deities (see discussion at 2:11-13). They also served the following deities: the gods of Aram (Syria), which are never mentioned by name; the gods of Sidon, which were Baal and Astarte; the gods of Moab, among whom was Chemosh of whom little is known (apparently he was a savage war god); the gods of the Ammonites,

---

[1] Keil and Delitzsch, *Joshua, Judges, Ruth*, p. 375.

among whom was Molech (cf. 1 Kings 11:5, 33), the worship of whom involved offering infant children by sacrificing them in fire; and the gods of the Philistines, a chief god being Dagon (16:23). Thus once again "the Israelites forsook the Lord and no longer served him" (10:6).

B. Servitude: Philistines and Ammonites (10:7–9)

1. *Affliction in Trans-Jordan* (10:7–8)

Because of their apostasy the Lord sold the Israelites into the hands of the Philistines and the Ammonites, who subjugated them for eighteen years. The Philistines are thought to originally have come from the Aegean Sea area, probably from Crete (called Caphtor at times). There was a major migration during the twelfth century B.C. in which they caused the downfall of the Hittite empire and also invaded Egypt. However, since the Philistines are mentioned earlier in the Old Testament (Gen. 21:32; 26:1; Exod. 13:17), it is understood that some of them migrated to the coastal area of Canaan much earlier than the twelfth century B.C. The Ammonites were descendants of Lot through his incestuous relationship with his daughter (Gen. 19:36–38). At one time the Ammonites controlled the territory between the Arnon and Jabbok rivers (Deut. 2:16–25; cf. Judg. 11:13) but were later displaced by the Amorites who in turn were defeated by Israel. The Ammonites were forced to move east of the Jabbok River.

Israel was thus afflicted on both sides: by the Philistines on the west and the Ammonites on the east. The severity of the affliction is seen in the terms "shattered and crushed" (10:8). The Hebrew term for "shattered" is used to describe the Lord's destruction of the Egyptians in the Red Sea (Exod. 15:6). The Hebrew word for "crushed" is applied elsewhere to a reed ("splintered," Isa. 36:6) and commonly has the figurative meaning of oppression (cf. Deut. 28:33; Isa. 58:6; Amos 4:1). The affliction continued for eighteen years, with the tribes of Reuben, Gad, and the half-tribe of Manasseh east of the Jordan suffering at the hands of the Ammonites.

2. *Affliction in central Canaan* (10:9)

Ultimately the Ammonites carried their warfare against Israel westward, crossing the Jordan and penetrating into the central and southern region to punish the tribes of Judah, Benjamin, and Ephraim.

C. Supplication (10:10–18)

1. *Remorse* (10:10)

Suffering from intense affliction, the Israelites cried to the Lord in repentance, confessing their sin of idolatry (cf. 3:9, 15: 4:3; 6:6–7).

2. *Reminder* (10:11–14)

Since the sinning cycles occurred so often, the Lord did not respond immediately. He reminded them of His past deliverances, but despite His faithfulness to them they continually turned away from Him and followed Baal. In rebuking the nation the Lord traced the history of His faithfulness: He delivered them from Egypt (Exod. 14); from the Amorites (Num. 21:21–35); from the Ammonites (Judg. 3:13–29); from the Philistines (Judg. 3:31); from the Sidonians (probably allied with Jabin since there is no specific reference; cf. Judg. 4:2–3); from the Amalekites (Exod. 17:8–15; Judg. 3:13–29); and from the Maonites.[2]

In spite of the Lord's help in the past, the nation had forsaken Him and served other gods; therefore He would no longer deliver them. In a statement of irony the Lord challenged them to appeal to the gods they had chosen for themselves (cf. Deut. 32:37–38; 2 Kings 3:13; Jer. 2:28). The rebuke was designed to provoke genuine repentance.

3. *Repentance* (10:15–18)

The rebuke had an effect on the nation whose repentance was demonstrated in four ways: (1) They acknowledged their sin to the Lord (10:15). (2) They acknowledged the Lord's prerogative in dealing with them according to His sovereign will (v. 15). (3) They removed the foreign gods from among them (v. 16). (4) They served the Lord. As a result the Lord could bear the suffering of Israel no longer and determined to help them.

Verses 17 and 18 are preparatory to Israel's deliverance through Jephthah and narrate the preparation for battle by the armies of Ammon and Israel. The Ammonites gathered in Gilead—that portion east of the Jordan over which they had obtained control; Israel prepared for battle at Mizpah ("watchtower"), which is probably synonymous with "Ramath-Mizpah" or "Ramoth-Gilead" (cf. Deut.

---

[2]The identification here is unclear. The Massoretic Text reads "Maon," while the Septuagint reads "Midian." The former may be a scribal error, although the reading is possible since the Maonites may be related to the Meunites who came from the same territory and are seen as Israel's enemies (1 Chron. 4:41; 2 Chron. 20:1; 26:7). Maon was located nine miles south of Hebron and inhabited by a small number of people.

4:43; Josh. 13:26; 1 Kings 4:13). Mizpah lay south of the Jabbok River in the territory of Gad.

Verse 18 in particular anticipates the judgeship of Jephthah. In Israel's preparation for battle with the Ammonites, they offered the leadership of the eastern tribes to the one who could launch the attack against their enemies.

D. Salvation: Jephthah (11:1–12:6)

1. *Rejection of Jephthah* (11:1–3)

The introduction to the story of Jephthah reveals the depravity of the period of the judges as well as the grace of God in times of crisis. The former is seen in that Jephthah, the son of a prostitute, was summoned to the leadership in Israel; the latter is reflected in the fact that Jesus Christ had a prostitute as an ancestor (Matt. 1:5) and yet delivered the world from the bondage of sin. Similarly, Jephthah would be used to deliver Israel from its bondage to the Ammonites.

Jephthah, as a descendant of Gilead, was of the tribe of Manasseh (cf. Num. 26:29–30; 27:1; 36:1). He was a "mighty warrior" (11:1; Hebrew, *gibbor*), a term also used to describe Gideon (6:12). The designation "mighty warrior" emphasizes the strength and vitality of the successful warrior. The exploits of these mighty men were occasions for delight and storytelling (cf. 1 Chron. 11:15–19). Originally the Hebrew word was a technical term denoting men of social class and nobles who bore arms for their king (cf. "man of standing," Ruth 2:1; 1 Sam. 9:1; "mighty men," 2 Kings 15:20 NASB).[3]

Because of Jephthah's inferior birth (he was probably a half-Canaanite), the true sons of Gilead drove him from the family home; they refused to let their half brother share in the family inheritance. It is possible in the light of Jephthah's aggressive qualities that his brothers both feared and resented him. Jephthah fled to the land of Tob, the area north of Gilead, where he gathered "a group of adventurers" around him (11:3). The designation in Hebrew is the same as for the men who surrounded Abimelech (see discussion at 9:4). First Samuel 22:2 offers some insight into the nature of these men: they were in distress, in debt, or discontented. These men followed Jephthah, which probably means they went out "upon warlike and predatory expeditions like the Bedouins."[4]

---

[3]John N. Oswalt, "גָּבַר," *Theological Wordbook*, vol. 1, p. 148.
[4]Keil and Delitzsch, *Joshua, Judges, Ruth*, p. 379.

2. *Solicitation of Jephthah* (11:4-11)

After a considerable period of time had elapsed and while the Israelites were at war with the Ammonites, the elders of Gilead summoned Jephthah, saying, "Come, be our commander, so we can fight the Ammonites" (11:6). It is apparent Jephthah had made a reputation for himself that encouraged his people to appoint him as their leader in battle. Jephthah expressed his astonishment at their request and apparently laid the blame for his expulsion from home on the elders of Gilead although his brothers were the guilty ones. The elders persisted in their request, promising to make Jephthah head over all who lived in Gilead (v. 8). When the elders repeated their promise, Jephthah acceded to their proposition and the people made him "head and commander" over them (v. 11). The term "head" (Hebrew, *ro'sh*) is very common, occurring nearly 750 times in the Old Testament. It is used to designate the head as the part of the body (Gen. 3:15) and, by extension, the chief of a family (Exod. 6:14) and chief officer of the divisions of Israel (Exod. 18:25).[5] Here the designation is more precise, meaning "a chief in war and peace."[6] The term commander (Hebrew, *qasin*) means a "commander in war,"[7] and it is used in Joshua 10:24.

> This word is a military term. It signifies the man responsible for recruiting, an administrator in the army. It appears to denote the one at the head (parallel to "head ones," Mic 3:1, 9) of an army (Josh 10:24), or people (i.e. as political ruler; cf. Isa 1:10; Mic 3:1).[8]

After the elders swore an oath invoking the Lord as witness (11:10), Jephthah and the elders confirmed the appointment at the central sanctuary at Mizpah with a solemn gathering of the people.

3. *Disputation with the Ammonites* (11:12-28)

a) *Exclamation of the Ammonites* (11:12-13)

Jephthah's diplomatic ability was clearly evident as he began negotiations with the Ammonites in demanding to know why they had attacked his country. The Ammonites responded by charging Israel with having taken their land between the Arnon and Jabbok rivers when they came up from Egypt. In fact, Israel had taken this land from Sihon, king of the Amorites (Num. 21:21-26). Sihon had previously

---

[5]William White, "רֹאשׁ," *Theological Wordbook*, vol. 1, p. 825.
[6]Keil and Delitzsch, *Joshua, Judges, Ruth*, p. 379.
[7]Brown, Driver, and Briggs, *Hebrew and English Lexicon*, p. 892.
[8]Gerard Van Groningen, "קָצִף," *Theological Wordbook*, vol. 2, p. 807.

taken the disputed land from Moab (Num. 21:26), and the Ammonites thought they had a legitimate claim to the land through their association with Moab.

b) *Explanation of Jephthah* (11:14–28)

Jephthah diplomatically answered the allegations of the Ammonites by tracing Israel's history in entering the land and showing that Israel had neither taken the land from the Ammonites nor the Moabites (11:15). After arriving at Kadesh Israel asked Edom and Moab for permission to pass through their territory. When the permission was not given Israel avoided traveling through Edom and Moab (Num. 20:14–21); instead, they skirted the lands of Edom and Moab and came to the east side of Moab (v. 18). From there Israel sent messengers to Sihon, king of the Amorites at Heshbon, requesting permission to pass through the land of the Amorites (v. 19). Instead of granting them permission, Sihon entered into warfare with them (v. 20). In the verses that follow, Jephthah revealed Israel's rightful claim to the land. (1) Israel took the land from Sihon in battle, giving them a legitimate claim to the land (v. 21). (2) Israel took the land from the Amorites, not the Ammonites (v. 22). (3) Since God had given the land to Israel by driving out the Amorites, the Ammonites had no legitimate claim to it (v. 23). The emphasis that God gave them the land is also seen in verse 21. (4) Jephthah suggested that Israel possessed what God had given them and the Ammonites possessed what their god had given them. Jephthah did not acknowledge the vailidity of the Ammonite god but in a statement of irony suggested that perhaps their god had been stingy (11:24)!

> Jephthah argues that the two deities had shown their will—Yahweh by giving Israel victory over Sihon, and Chemosh by not enabling Moab to resist Sihon's earlier encroachments. In either case the divine will must be accepted as a *fait accompli*. The very fact that Yahweh had done more for Israel than Chemosh had been able to do for Moab proved the superior power of Yahweh.[9]

It is uncertain why Jephthah mentioned Chemosh, the god of the Moabites, rather than Milcom, who was the god of the Ammonites. One suggestion is that the Moabites were allied with Ammon in the battle; still another suggestion is that there was "a wide diffusion of the worship of the various deities."[10] The name Chemosh appears on the

---

[9]Bruce, "Judges," NBC, p. 268.
[10]Cundall and Morris, *Judges and Ruth*, p. 144.

famous Moabite Stone, which describes Ammon's dispute with Israel during the reign of Omri.[11]

Jephthah reminded the Ammonites that even Moab, when they heard of Israel's conquest of Sihon, feared Israel and did not attempt to regain their land that had previously been taken from them by Sihon (cf. Num. 22:2–4). Balak had refused to fight Israel. Did the Ammonites think they were better than Balak (11:25)? It had been three hundred years since Israel had captured the city of Heshbon from Sihon (11:26; Num. 21:25). Why had not the Ammonites laid claim before this?

Jephthah's statement in 11:26 is significant in that it confirms the early date of the Exodus as 1406 B.C. The following chronology traces the dating from the Exodus to the firm date of 966 B.C. (fourth year of Solomon's reign) as approximating 480 years: Exodus to Heshbon, 38 years; Heshbon to Jephthah, 300 years; remainder of Jephthah, 5 years; Samson, 40 years; Eli, 20 years; Samuel, 20 years; Saul, 15 years, David, 40 years; Solomon, 4 years.[12]

The final statement of this section indicates the necessity for the war between Israel and the Ammonites since the king of Ammon "paid no attention to the message Jephthah sent him" (11:28).

4. Subjugation of the Ammonites (11:29–33)

The Spirit of the Lord came upon Jephthah to empower him in his battle with the Ammonites. Gathering his men from Tob, Jephthah traveled southwest, passing through Manasseh to Mizpah. As Jephthah was going up to fight the Ammonites, he decided to make a serious vow at great expense in order to invoke the Lord's blessing and to ensure the victory in battle. Thus Jephthah vowed that he would give to the Lord and offer as a burnt offering whatever he would meet coming out the door of his house on his return from battle (for other serious vows, cf. Gen 28:20–22; 1 Sam. 1:11; 2 Sam. 15:7–9). Some commentators suggest that Jephthah had a human sacrifice in mind when he made his vow and compare Jephthah with the king of Moab (2 Kings 3:26–27). However, it should be remembered that the plan of Iron Age houses accommodated livestock as well as family.[13] Jephthah could have had an animal sacrifice in mind.

---

[11]Jack Finegan, *Light From the Ancient Past* (Princeton: Princeton University Press, 1959), pp. 188–89.

[12]Merrill F. Unger, *Introductory Guide to the Old Testament* (Grand Rapids: Zondervan Publishing House, 1951), p. 289; Davis, *Conquest and Crisis*, pp. 18, 124.

[13]Boling, *Judges*, AB, p. 208.

The Lord enabled Jephthah to decisively defeat the Ammonites, and "he devastated twenty towns from Aroer to the vicinity of Minnith, as far as Abel Keramim" (11:33). Aroer lay immediately north of the Arnon River; Minnith and Abel Keramim are unidentified. The last phrase of verse 33 provides a summary statement of Jephthah's war with the Ammonites: "Thus Israel subdued Ammon."

5. Realization of the vow of Jephthah (11:34–40)

The nature of Jephthah's vow remains a perplexing problem. Numerous commentators suggest Jephthah intended a human sacrifice and actually sacrificed his daughter as a burnt offering; others suggest that Jephthah committed his daughter to perpetual virginity through life-long service at the tabernacle. Cogent arguments support both views.[14] The following arguments favor the view that Jephthah offered his daughter in perpetual tabernacle service: (1) The text emphasizes her perpetual virginity (11:37–39). His daughter and her companions wept because of her virginity, and the result was that "she had no relations with a man" (NASB). (2) Child sacrifice was contrary to the Mosaic Law and virtually nonexistent in Israel (Lev. 18:21; 20:2–5; Deut. 12:31).

> Human sacrifice was always understood, from the days of Abraham (for whose son Isaac a ram was substituted by God) to be an offense and an abomination to Jehovah, being expressly denounced and forbidden . . . There is no evidence that any Israelite ever offered human sacrifice prior to the days of Ahaz (743–728 B.C.). It is inconceivable that God-fearing Jephthah could have supposed he would please the Lord by perpetrating such a crime and abomination.[15]

(3) The conjunction in 11:31 can be translated "or," suggesting a distinction between the two phrases as follows: "it shall be the LORD'S, or I will offer it up as a burnt offering" (NASB). Jephthah may well have been thinking of the law concerning vows in Leviticus 27. If he met a human being on his return, he would follow the law according to verses 1–8. In the case of his daughter, she could be committed to lifelong service in the tabernacle; if he met another human, he could redeem the individual at the appropriate price. If the vow involved an unclean animal, it would be sold; if a suitable animal were involved, it would be

---

[14]For a detailed discussion of both views, see Davis, *Conquest and Crisis*, pp. 124–28, and Wood, *Distressing Days*, pp. 288–95.

[15]Gleason L Archer, Jr., *A Survey of Old Testament Introduction* (Chicago: Moody, 1964), p. 267.

sacrificed.[16] (4) It would have been impossible for Jephthah to sacrifice his daughter as a burnt offering according to the law. Keil and Delitzsch note that

> burnt-offerings, that is to say bleeding burnt-offerings, in which the victim was slaughtered and burnt upon the altar, could only be offered upon the lawful altar at the tabernacle, or before the ark, through the medium of the Levitical priests, unless the sacrifice itself had been occasioned by some extraordinary manifestation of God; and that we cannot for a moment think of here. But is it credible that a priest or the priesthood should have consented to offer a sacrifice upon the altar of Jehovah which was denounced in the law as the greatest abomination of the heathen?[17]

(5) Jephthah knew the law well; it is inconceivable that a man so well acquainted with the law (cf. 11:15–27) would commit an act so contrary to the law. To argue that Jephthah did not know the law does not agree with Jephthah's knowledge as observed in the above passage. (6) Jephthah was approved by God in Samuel's address to the nation (1 Sam. 12:11) and in the list of the heroes of faith (Heb. 11:32). (7) There is no indication that Jephthah responded in a rash manner. His negotiations with the Ammonites demonstrates his logical approach. (8) There is no clear statement suggesting that Jephthah offered his daughter as a burnt offering; instead, the statement "he did to her as he had vowed" seems to be explained more fully in the next sentence, "And she was a virgin" (11:39). The latter phrase would be meaningless if she was sacrificed. (9) Jephthah lamented the situation because his lineage was terminated through the perpetual virginity of his daughter and because she was an only child (11:34). (10) Israelite women served in the tabernacle and temple in cleaning or as doorkeepers (cf. Exod. 38:8; 1 Sam. 2:22).

The following arguments favor the view that Jephthah offered his daughter as a burnt offering in death: (1) The text seems to suggest this (11:31). The Hebrew word *olah* in its normal usage indicates a sacrificial offering.[18] (2) Jephthah expressed grief when his daughter met him; the text suggests he was about to lose his only child (vv. 34–35). (3) Jephthah was the son of a prostitute and could have assimilated heathen beliefs into his life (11:1–3), particularly since he lived with a gang of renegades in Tob. The king of Moab offered his oldest son as a

---

[16]Wood, *Distressing Days*, pp. 293–94.
[17]Keil and Delitzsch, *Joshua, Judges, Ruth*, pp. 393–94.
[18]Brown, Driver, and Briggs, *Hebrew and English Lexicon*, p. 750.

burnt offering (2 Kings 3:26–27). (4) Since Jephthah was the son of a prostitute and lived with ruthless men, he may have been ignorant of the Mosaic Law and not realized that child sacrifice was forbidden. (5) Jephthah made a thoughtless vow, dictated by the need to achieve a victory in battle. (6) The text indicates that Jephthah fulfilled his vow (11:39). (7) The young women of Israel commemorated the daughter of Jephthah annually (v. 40).

The major problem in adopting the view that Jephthah's daughter was committed to perpetual virginity in tabernacle service is the normal usage of the Hebrew word for burnt offering in 11:31. The Hebrew word usually refers to a sacrifice. This may be answered by recognizing that in the life of the nation Israel a burnt offering was not thought of in terms of a human being; rather, a burnt offering was in relation to an animal being offered to God in worship. A burnt offering was rarely found in relation to humans, and only to foreign gods, but not to the Lord.[19] Human sacrifice was not prevalent among Canaanites.[20] Moreover, if Jephthah had attempted to sacrifice his daughter, the problem remains that the priest would have been the one to actually carry out the sacrifice. It is unthinkable that a priest of Israel would have submitted himself to this heathen rite.

While the text is clearly an interpretive problem, there appear to be more problems in suggesting Jephthah sacrificed his daughter as a burnt offering. While the word *olah* normally means burnt offering, it is also normally used in Israelite culture as an animal offering. Moreover, Jephthah appears to have been acquainted with the law inasmuch as he was able to clearly rehearse Israel's history (11:12–28). Furthermore, Jephthah did not make a rash vow—he is seen as a logical man—and had the blessing of the Lord in giving him the victory and later in being listed as a hero of faith. This would have been inconceivable if he had actually sacrificed his daughter. It appears to be less problematic to suggest that Jephthah offered his daughter in tabernacle service, demanding perpetual virginity.

6. *Dissension with the Ephraimites* (12:1–6)

a) *Discussion with Ephraim* (12:1–3)

The dissension and chaos described in chapter 12 remind one of the theme of Judges: "In those days Israel had no king; everyone did as he

---

[19]Brown, Driver, and Briggs, *Hebrew and English Lexicon*, p. 750.
[20]G. Lloyd Carr, "עָלָה," *Theological Wordbook*, vol. 2, p. 668.

saw fit" (21:25). Because the men of Ephraim were jealous of Jephthah's victory (and, no doubt, coveted the spoils of war), they marshaled their forces and crossed the Jordan to Zaphon to threaten Jephthah. Zaphon was north of Succoth near Wadi Rajeb. They accused Jephthah of failing to summon them to war against the Ammonites, an action reminiscent of their anger with Gideon (8:1). In their anger they threatened to burn Jephthah's house (cf. 14:15; 15:6), which should also be understood as a threat on Jephthah's life.

Jephthah's response stands in contrast to that of Gideon. The latter placated the Ephraimites with soothing and congratulatory words (8:2–3); Jephthah, however, confronted the Ephraimites with both words and action. He reminded them of the long-standing Ammonite oppression (12:2; cf. 10:7–8); furthermore, he had indeed called them for assistance—an event not directly recorded in Scripture but which may have taken place when he was preparing for war as he passed through Mizpah opposite Ephraim (11:29). Having failed to receive help from the Ephraimites, Jephthah recalled, "I took my life in my hands" (12:3; a Hebrew idiom emphasizing the risk he took in fighting the Ammonites). Jephthah concluded the confrontation by challenging the validity of their charge against him.

b) *Devastation of Ephraim* (12:4–6)

The Ephraimites further provoked the Israelites living on the east side of the Jordan River by suggesting they were refugees or deserters from the tribes of Ephraim and Manasseh. The charge led to war. Jephthah gathered his army and defeated the Ephraimites. He captured the fords of the Jordan, preventing the defeated Ephraimites from escaping to their tribal territory. Whenever an Ephraimite warrior attempted to cross the Jordan, the Gileadites guarding the ford tested him by asking him to pronounce "Shibboleth," meaning an ear of corn. When the Ephraimite said, "Sibboleth," he was seized and killed.

> The Ephraimite dialect appears to have been similar to that of the Amorites and Arabs, with *s* taking the place of *sh*, so their approximation of *Sibboleth* immediately revealed their identity and led to their execution.[21]

The result of this intriguing procedure was the death of forty-two thousand Ephraimites.

---

[21]Cundall and Morris, *Judges and Ruth*, p. 151.

E. Silence: thirty-one years (12:7–15)

1. *Judgeship of Jephthah* (12:7)

Jephthah was a judge of Israel for six years. Probably his work was only east of the Jordan, and this was partly because of his conflict with the Ephraimites. At his death he was buried in a town of Gilead.

2. *Judgeship of Ibzan* (12:8–10)

Apart from the comments in these verses, nothing is known of Ibzan. His large family of sixty children indicates a multiplicity of wives and reflects his status and position of prominence in the community. By contracting marriages outside the family clan, Ibzan probably sought to increase his sphere of influence. Ibzan led Israel for seven years and was buried in Bethlehem. Since the Bethlehem in Judah is normally designated "Bethlehem of Judah" or "Bethlehem Ephratah," the Bethlehem mentioned here was probably located in Zebulun (cf. Josh. 19:15).

3. *Judgeship of Elon* (12:11–12)

Elon, who was of Zebulun, bore the name of a family clan (cf. Gen. 46:14; Num. 26:26). He led Israel ten years and was buried in Aijalon in the territory of Zebulun. The Aijalon mentioned here is to be distinguished from the Valley of Aijalon in Dan, the place where Joshua defeated the Amorites (Josh. 10:12).

4. *Judgeship of Abdon* (12:13–15)

Abdon was from Pirathon, six miles southwest of Shechem in the territory of Ephraim. Once more the text emphasizes the prominence and wealth of the judge, for Abdon had forty sons and thirty grandsons (not nephews as in KJV), all of whom had their own donkeys (cf. 10:4; 2 Sam. 13:29; 16:2). The mention of the Amalekites may suggest there were still pockets of the marauders in the southern locality.

For Further Study

1. Read an article on Jephthah in a Bible dictionary or encyclopedia.

2. Analyze the life of Jephthah. What kind of a man was he? What were his strengths? his weaknesses?

3. Contrast the lives of Gideon and Jephthah.

4. Study the vow of Jephthah. Was it necessary for him to make the vow? Should he have kept the vow?

Chapter 8

Seventh Cycle of Oppression
(Judges 13:1–16:31)

A major invasion by the Philistines occurred about 1200 B.C. when these sea people settled along the Canaanite coast. The cities of Ashdod, Gaza, Ashkelon, Gath, and Ekron became the five principal cities of the Philistines (cf. 1 Sam. 6:17). Following the conquest of the coastal area, the Philistines began to move inland and Israel felt the oppressive force of the militarily superior Philistines.

To counteract the Philistine invasion, the Lord raised up a major judge, Samson, to lead the people. Samson was an unusual judge in that while he was mightily used of God to defeat the Philistines in numerous skirmishes he was nonetheless a carnal man who functioned according to his viscerogenic desires.

The judgeship of Samson brings the chronology of Judges to an end; in fact, there is an overlap of the judgeship of Samson and the ministry of Samuel. Leon Wood places the twenty-year ministry of Samson at 1075 to 1055 B.C.[1]

A. Sin: apostasy (13:1a)

The reason Israel was oppressed by the Philistine invaders is stated in the opening verse of the life of Samson. Israel again apostatized into idolatrous worship.

B. Servitude: Philistines (13:1b)

As a result of apostasy, Israel was delivered by the Lord into the hands of the Philistines for forty years. This was the longest oppression of Israel by any one group. Since the Philistines oppressed Israel for

---

[1]Wood, *Distressing Days*, p. 14.

forty years and Samson led Israel for twenty years, it is apparent that Samson began his judgeship while still a teenager, for the Philistines still ruled Israel at his death. The Philistines were ultimately conquered at the battle of Mizpah (1 Sam. 7:5–14).

C. Salvation: Samson (13:2–16:31)

1. *Birth of Samson* (13:2–25)

a) *Annunciation of the angel* (13:2–5)

1) *Annunciation of the birth* (13:2–3). Zorah was located seventeen miles west of Jerusalem on the border of Dan and Judah in Philistine territory. The deliverer whom God raised up was from the area that had experienced the oppression of the Philistines. The wife of Manoah ("rest") was from the clan of the Danites and was sterile (cf. 1 Sam. 1:2; Luke 1:7). This barrenness was viewed as a tragedy because she was beyond human help and could not continue the family line. However, her frustration was about to be ended. The angel of the Lord, a theophany, appeared to Manoah's wife and announced that she would conceive and have a son. The angel of the Lord brought a similar message in announcing the birth of Isaac (Gen. 18:10), and an angel also announced the birth of John the Baptist (Luke 1:13).

2) *Annunciation of the Nazirite vow* (13:4–5a). The angel of the Lord announced that the son would be a Nazirite, obligated to abide by the law of the Nazirite vow (Num. 6:1–8). The Nazirite vow was usually voluntary and for a specified period of time; occasionally it was for life as in the case of Samson. The designation Nazirite ("devoted" or "consecrated") involved obeying several major prohibitions by which the person indicated his devotion to the Lord. (1) He could not drink "wine" or "fermented drink" (13:4; Num. 6:3–4). The Hebrew term for "fermented drink" is variously translated. The term is usually used in an unfavorable sense ("drinks," Isa. 5:11, 22; "beer," Isa. 28:7; 56:12; Mic. 2:11; Prov. 20:1); the term refers to beverages forbidden to priests on duty ("fermented drink" Lev. 10:9), rulers ("beer," Prov. 31:4), and Nazirites ("fermented drink," Num. 6:3). The term refers also to common beverages ("fermented drink," Deut. 14:26; 29:6) and also to the beverage used in libation offerings ("fermented drink," Num. 28:7).[2] Since there was no distilled liquor in Bible times, the Hebrew term may refer to any alcoholic drink of fermented grain or fruit such as

---

[2]Brown, Driver, and Briggs, *Hebrew and English Lexicon*, p. 1016; Victor P. Hamilton, "שֵׁכָר," *Theological Wordbook*, vol. 2, p. 926.

beer.[3] (2) The Nazirite was prohibited from cutting his hair for the duration of the vow (Num. 6:5). (3) The Nazirite was not to go near a dead person (Num. 6:6).

The angel of the Lord cited an additional prohibition in that the son was not to eat any unclean thing (13:4). This may be a reference to the dietary obligations of the Israelites (Lev. 11; Deut. 14), or it may also include the prohibition of eating anything that came from the grapevine (Num. 6:4).

3) *Annunciation of the deliverance* (13:5b). The angel of the Lord announced the purpose of the boy being set apart as a Nazirite: he would begin to deliver Israel from the hands of the Philistines. The statement "he will begin the deliverance" may suggest that Samson's work in freeing Israel from the Philistines would be incomplete. Subjugation of the Philistines was not completed until the reign of David (1 Chron. 18:1).

b) *Declaration of the woman* (13:6-7)

In relating the incident to her husband, the woman said that "a man of God" had appeared to her (13:6). The term man of God was usually understood as a prophet (cf. 1 Sam. 9:6-9). The woman, however, recognized the uniqueness of the man of God and further described him as having an appearance "like an angel of God," meaning he inspired reverence, godly fear, and awe.[4] In her excitement the woman neglected to ask the man where he had come from. She was jubilant at the prospect of motherhood and informed her husband that she would bear a son who would be a Nazirite for the duration of his life. The woman failed, however, to mention that her son would deliver Israel from the Philistines. Did she not believe it at this point?

c) *Affirmation of the angel* (13:8-23)

1) *Reappearance* (13:8-14). Manoah believed his wife's story and prayed to the Lord that the man of God might reappear in order to teach them how to bring up the boy. The Lord answered Manoah's prayer and the angel of God reappeared to the woman while she was in the field (13:9). The woman quickly went to her husband and led him to the angel. When Manoah was assured that the messenger was the same one who had appeared to his wife, he inquired about the fulfillment of the prophecy and the nature of the boy's work (v. 12). The angel repeated the instructions he had given to the woman, and emphasized

[3]Boling, *Judges*, AB, p. 219.
[4]Brown, Driver, and Briggs, *Hebrew and English Lexicon*, p. 431.

that not only was the boy to abide by the Nazirite regulations, but the woman was not to eat anything from the grapevine or any unclean food; and she was not to drink wine or any other fermented drink (v. 14). The prohibition for the woman, no doubt, was given because the boy was a Nazirite from the womb (v. 5).

2) *Reverence* (13:15–19). In appreciation Manoah wanted to prepare a meal for the man of God by killing a goat. A leisurely meal was a common symbol of hospitality and fellowship (cf. Gen 18:3–8; note also the similarity with the story of Gideon, 6:19). The angel, however, declined the invitation and instructed Manoah to offer a burnt offering to the Lord. The explanatory phrase: "Manoah did not realize that it was the angel of the Lord" (13:16) perhaps suggests the burnt offering was to be made for the angel of the Lord. The burnt offering was the most common of the Old Testament sacrifices in which the worshiper acknowledged his guilt and the necessity of shedding blood for the atonement of sins. The offering also signified the total surrender and dedication of the worshiper to the Lord.[5]

Manoah still only comprehended the messenger as a prophet. Desiring to honor him Manoah therefore asked him his name so that when the event came to pass the messenger could be accorded the proper honor (13:17). The angel refused to answer the request of Manoah, reminding him of the incomprehensible nature of his name: "Why do you ask my name? It is beyond understanding (13:18; "wonderful," NASB). The term "beyond understanding" (Hebrew, *pil'i*) most often refers to the acts of God and indicates acts that are unusual and beyond human capabilities.[6] The thought is expressed in Psalm 139:6. The noun is used as a title of Messiah in Isaiah 9:6.

Manoah then offered the goat along with the grain offering (Lev. 2) on a rock that became an altar of worship for the couple. The concluding statement that "the Lord did an amazing thing" (13:19) is explained by verse 20, which says the angel ascended toward heaven in the flame from the altar.

3) *Disappearance* (13:20–23). The fire that consumed the offering on the altar indicated God's acceptance of the offering as in the case of Gideon (6:21); moreover, the fire symbolized the shekinah glory of God

---

[5]For a helpful discussion of the burnt offering see G. J. Wenham, *The Book of Leviticus* in ICC (Grand Rapids: Eerdmans, 1979), pp. 47–66; for a classic discussion of the meaning and typology of the offerings see Andrew Jukes, *The Law of the Offerings* (Grand Rapids: Kregel, reprint, n.d.).

[6]Victor P. Hamilton, "פָּלָא," *Theological Wordbook*, vol. 2, p. 723.

(cf. Exod. 3:2–6). Realizing now that the messenger had been a manifestation of God, the couple prostrated themselves in fear and worship. They realized that they had seen evidence of God's presence and were fearful that they would die, for no one could see God and live (Exod. 33:20). Manoah's wife reminded her husband that the acceptance of their offering was a sign they would not die.

d) *Origination of Samson* (13:24–25)

Manoah's wife gave birth to a son and named him Samson, probably meaning sun. Since they lived near Beth Shemesh ("house of the sun"), the shrine of the sun-god, Samson's name may have been derived from this local town, although it is recognized that his parents were not idolaters. Josephus suggests it means "one that is *strong*."[7] Anticipating the events that follow, the narrator notes that Samson grew and the blessing of the Lord was on him.

The statement that "the Spirit of the LORD began to stir him" (13:25) refers to the Spirit enduing Samson with power for service. The reference in Samson's case is to physical strength; hence it appears that Samson began to receive his supernatural strength at this point. Samson's home at the time was Mahaneh Dan ("camp of Dan") in the Valley of Sorek between Zorah and Eshtaol.

2. *Marriage of Samson* (14:1–20)

a) *Seeking a Canaanite wife from Timnah* (14:1–4)

The first of Samson's wives came from Timnah, four miles southwest of Beth Shemesh on the southern side of the Valley of Sorek. Although the town was on the border of Judah and Dan and belonged to the tribe of Dan (Josh. 19:43), it was occupied by the Philistines at this time; nonetheless, there was free movement into Philistine territory.

As Samson returned from Timnah he announced, "I have seen a Philistine woman in Timnah; now get her for me as my wife" (14:2). According to Eastern custom, marriage was negotiated and arranged by the parents (cf. Gen. 34:4; 38:6). Samson's parents objected to the intended marriage since they were aware that the Mosaic Law prohibited Israelite marriages with foreigners (Gen. 24:3–4; 26:34–35; Deut. 7:3). Their designation of the Philistines as uncircumcised was a term of derision (cf. 15:18; 1 Sam. 14:6; 17:26, 36; 31:4; 1 Chron. 10:4). Circumcision was practiced by the Egyptians and Semites, and it appears

---

[7]Flavius Josephus, *The Antiquities of the Jews* in *Josephus Complete Works*, trans. William Whiston (Grand Rapids: Kregel, 1960), V. 8. 4.

the Philistines were the only group that did not practice it. When Samson's parents exhorted him to find a wife among the Hebrew people, he appealed to his father (14:3). It is noteworthy that Samson's only criterion for a wife was "she looks good to me" (NASB). It was a superficial basis for selecting a wife; if Samson used the proper method, then Hollywood should have the happiest marriages!

The statement of 14:4 is parenthetical. While Samson was responsible for his disobedience to the Mosaic Law in marrying a non-Hebrew, the Lord would sovereignly use the occasion to confront the Philistines.[8] Because of his marriage to the Philistine woman, Samson's exploits against the Philistines would begin and would generally nullify the oppressive measures of the Philistines. The final statement of verse 4 indicates the necessity of Samson's countermeasures: "for at that time they (the Philistines) were ruling over Israel."

b) *Sojourning to Timnah* (14:5–9)

Although Samson was a carnal man, God nonetheless used him as a judge of the Philistines. On this occasion he was going down to Timnah with his parents, no doubt to contract his marriage to the Philistine woman. During the journey Samson became temporarily separated from his parents and suddenly met a lion. The Spirit of the Lord came upon Samson, giving him unusual physical strength so that he "tore" the lion as easily as if it had been a goat (14:6)! "Tore" is from the Hebrew verb *shisa*, which is in the intensive piel stem; the piel stem also is found in Leviticus 1:17 where the priest tears a bird by (or at) the wings. The indication is that Samson split the lion in two by pulling the hind legs apart in the manner in which a carcass is torn at a Semitic meal. The statement that Samson did not tell his parents what happened anticipates the event that follows.

Verse 7 appears to describe a later visit to Timnah. The earlier opinion that Samson held concerning the woman was confirmed by this later visit: Literally, the text says, "She was right in Samson's eyes." As Samson was returning, he stopped by the place where he had killed the lion and discovered that a swarm of bees had built a honeycomb. Under ordinary circumstances bees would not approach a decomposing carcass. In the dry heat of Palestine the moisture of a corpse evaporates so quickly that the corpse does not undergo normal decay but dries out and becomes mummified. When Samson discovered the honey in the

---

[8]See discussion on 9:23.

carcass, "he scraped the honey into his hands" (14:9 NASB). The Hebrew verb is picturesque, suggesting "to draw out" as bread is drawn
out of the oven and put into the basket.[9] Although many commentators suggest Samson broke the Nazirite vow by touching the carcass
of an animal, an examination of the biblical passages emphasizes the
prohibition relates to the corpse of a person, not an animal (Num.
6:6–12; 19:11–19). Otherwise a priest, who had similar prohibitions,
would have violated the law each time he presented a sacrificial offering (Lev. 21:1–3). Although Samson gave his parents some of the
honey, he avoided telling them where it came from; perhaps he had
already determined to tell the riddle and did not want anyone to
know it.

c) *Celebrating the wedding feast of Timnah* (14:10–14)

Samson's father went down to Timnah, probably to agree to the
marriage in behalf of Samson. Samson, meanwhile, fulfilled his obligation as a bridegroom by preparing a marriage feast, which was customary for the bridegroom. The word "feast" (Hebrew, *mishteh*) has a
basic meaning of "banquet, occasion for drinking, drinking-bout."[10] In
its literal use it may indicate a wedding feast (14:10; Gen. 29:22) or a
banquet where the guests became drunk (1 Sam. 25:36); in its figurative sense it may set forth messianic blessings (Isa. 25:6). Since such a
banquet would normally involve the bridegroom in drinking wine (cf.
John 2:1–11), it seems apparent that Samson broke his Nazirite vow
(Num. 6:3).

It is evident that this was not a Hebrew wedding since the Philistines
invited thirty companions for Samson. These were synonymous with
the "attendants of the bridegroom" (Matt. 9:15 NASB).

At the feast Samson proposed a riddle, which was an old custom,
particularly in ancient Greece. "Such tests of wits are a feature of social
life in non-literate societies, as among the Arab peasants and Bedouin."[11] The stakes were high: if the Philistines could solve Samson's
riddle within the seven days of the wedding feast, they would receive
from him "thirty linen garments and thirty sets of clothes." The linen
garments were costly pieces of fine material that were worn either next
to the skin or as an outer garment. The thirty "sets of clothes" were not
ordinary, everyday clothes; rather, these garments were worn on festal

---

[9]Cassel, "The Book of Judges," Lange's, p. 196.
[10]Brown, Driver, and Briggs, *Hebrew and English Lexicon*, p. 1059.
[11]Gray, *Joshua, Judges and Ruth*, CB, p. 350.

occasions and were often decorated with fine embroidery (Gen. 45:22; 2 Kings 5:5).

When the Philistines demanded to hear the riddle, Samson responded, "Out of the eater, something to eat; out of the strong, something sweet" (14:14). Although the Philistines thought about Samson's words for three days, they could not discover their meaning.

d) *Securing the riddle's answer from Samson* (14:15–18)

This section points to Samson's weakness regarding women. Samson's disclosure of the riddle while under his wife's pressure anticipates his telling Delilah the secret of his strength.

When the wedding guests discovered they could not solve the riddle, they approached Samson's wife and threatened her, saying, "Coax your husband into explaining the riddle for us" (14:15). *Patah*, the Hebrew word for "coax" ("entice," NASB), has a root meaning of "be simple" and "might relate to the immature or simple one who is open to all kinds of enticement, not having developed a discriminating judgment as to what is right or wrong."[12] The intensive verb form (piel) is used of seducing a virgin (Exod. 22:16), enticing a man to sin (Prov. 1:10), and deceiving someone (2 Sam. 3:25; Prov. 24:28). The same Hebrew word is used in 16:5 where the Philistines provoked Delilah to "lure," or entice, Samson; the term points to the gullibility of Samson, particularly where a woman was concerned.

The seriousness of the Philistine threat is seen in the warning "or we will burn you and your father's household to death" (14:15). The question "Did you invite us here to rob us?" (v. 15) suggests the Philistines thought the woman was part of a plot to take away their land. The Philistines thus warned her that their occupation of the land was being threatened by Samson's presence. As a result Samson's wife resorted to the best weapons she knew of to gain the answer to Samson's secret— tears and a charge that he did not love her! (v. 16). The NIV correctly reports the emphasis: "Then Samson's wife threw herself on him" rather than "wept before him" (NASB). Although Samson reminded her that he had not even told his parents the riddle, she kept up the pressure by appealing to him through tears for seven days. Recognizing her dilemma on the seventh and final day, she intensified the pressure (v. 17). When Samson could withstand the pressure no longer, he told his wife his secret. She immediately told the Philistines.

---

[12]Goldberg, "פָּתָה," *Theological Wordbook*, vol. 2, p. 742.

At the last moment—before sunset—the men of the town (i.e., the thirty companions, 14:11) approached Samson and provided the solution to the riddle (v. 18). Samson responded with a poem of his own as he immediately realized that his wife had deceived him. The reference to a heifer reveals Samson's anger at his wife—it was not exactly a fitting term for a wife at her wedding party!

e) *Slaughtering thirty men at Ashkelon* (14:19)

The Spirit of the Lord again came upon Samson, providing him with unusual strength. He went down to Ashkelon, a principal city of the Philistines that was twenty-three miles southwest of Timnah on the Mediterranean coast.[13] Samson wanted to avoid extracting his "dues" from anyone who would be connected with the wedding. He killed thirty Philistines at Ashkelon, took their clothes, and presented them to the men who had won the wager. The conquest of the thirty Philistines should be understood as the first stage of the fulfillment of 14:4. The Lord was beginning to deliver Israel from the power of the Philistines.

Samson was so angry with his new bride that he went directly home after paying his debt. He left his bride at the wedding feast. Their marriage had not yet been consummated after the seven feast days when she disclosed the solution to Samson's riddle to the Philistines. However, Samson was so angry at his bride that he scorned her; he chose to return to his parental home rather than consummate the marriage. Thus he openly rejected his wife.

f) *Summation of the wedding* (14:20)

Since the bride was placed in an embarrassing position at the wedding feast, she was given "to the friend who had attended him (Samson) at his wedding." This was the "best man" (for a similar expression see John 3:29 where John the Baptist is seen as the friend of Christ, the Bridegroom).

3. *Exploits of Samson* (15:1–16:3)

a) *Philistine crop destroyed* (15:1–8)

1) *Return of Samson* (15:1–2). When Samson's anger abated, he returned to his wife. The occasion was during the time of the wheat harvest in May; so not much time had elapsed following the wedding

---

[13]See Garstang, *Joshua-Judges*, for an illustration of the fortress, page 286, for a plan of the city, page 358, and for a discussion of the city and the archaeological work, pages 336–37.

feast inasmuch as most Palestinian weddings took place in the spring. Samson brought his wife a goat as a present, a common custom for that time (cf. Gen. 38:17). The goat was probably not a present to establish a reconciliation as some suggest; instead, it was the gift of the visiting husband in a *sadika* ("lover" or "mistress") marriage. This is similar to a form of marriage found among Palestinian Arabs in which there is no permanent cohabitation. The woman is mistress in her own home while the husband, who is known as *joz musarrib* ("a visiting husband") comes to his wife as a guest and brings her presents.[14]

When Samson wanted to enter his wife's room, her father prevented him from doing so. He explained, "I was so sure you thoroughly hated her" (15:2). The word "hate" (Hebrew, *sane*) is the same term used in the divorce formula (Deut. 24:3). As a result the father had given his daughter to Samson's friend. In order to pacify Samson the father offered him his younger daughter instead.

2) *Rage of Samson* (15:3). Samson felt an injustice had been done to him when his wife's father gave her to another man; Samson would not be held accountable for what he would do. Retribution was about to be unleashed on the Philistines!

3) *Revenge of Samson* (15:4–5). The Hebrew term translated "foxes" can also refer to jackals, which are common to Palestine and are more readily caught than foxes since jackals run in packs. Samson took them in pairs, tied their tails together with a torch in between, and released them to run in the Philistine grain fields. The jackals that were tied together ran wildly through the grainfields, because of their natural fear of fire as well as the pain of being burned. Both the "shocks" and the "standing grain" were consumed. Since this was the dry season, the grain burned swiftly as three hundred jackals ran in all directions. Even the vineyards and olive groves were burned.

The concept of setting foxes ablaze by their tails was not new. The fox was called *lampouris* in Greek, meaning bright, burning tail. The Romans had a custom at the festival of Cerealia (feast of the corn-goddess) of attaching torches to the tails of the foxes in such a way that the flames ultimately consumed the animals.

> The idea of the ceremony was undoubtedly to present the fox, who, according to the story, once set the grain-fields on fire, as a propitiatory offering to ward off mildew, of which he is a type.[15]

---

[14]de Vaux, *Ancient Israel*, vol. 1, p. 29.
[15]Cassel, "The Book of Judges," p. 205.

Burning the grain of an enemy was sometimes used for revenge (cf. 2 Sam. 14:28–33). The Philistines lost valuable crops through the disaster; they were discovering that Samson, the deliverer, was a man to be reckoned with.

4) *Revenge of the Philistines* (15:6–8). The Philistines soon heard that Samson was responsible for their enormous crop losses and that he had attacked them to compensate for the loss of his wife. They countered by approaching the home of Samson's wife and burned both her and her father to death.

A seemingly endless cycle was now established. When Samson heard of the death of his wife, he determined to take further revenge on the Philistines. "He attacked them viciously and slaughtered many of them" (15:8). The word "viciously" in the literal Hebrew is "leg on thigh," an idiom understood in various ways. It may be a wrestling term or simply a savage slaughter in which the victims are piled on one another. It is possible that Samson saw himself as a blood avenger (Lev. 24:17–21).

Following this latest encounter with the Philistines, Samson went down and lived in a cave in the rock of Etam (15:8). Etam was located about two miles southwest of Bethlehem. "It was a cave in the cliffs above the Wady Isma'in, which was accessible only by descending through a fissure in the cliff-face, wide enough for one person to pass through at a time."[16]

b) *Philistine contingent destroyed* (15:9–20)

1) *Samson seized by the men of Judah* (15:9–13). This section illustrates the condition of Israel at that time. Under bondage to the Philistines, the Israelites were afraid that Samson would bring trouble on them because he had infuriated the Philistines. Hence, the men of Judah determined to hand Samson over to the Philistines.

The indication is that a large contingent of Philistines camped near Lehi in Judah, frightening the people of Judah (15:9). Lehi, located near Beth Shemesh, means "jawbone" and was so named because of the appearance of the rock. Fearing a confrontation with the Philistines, the men of Judah approached the cave where Samson was hiding and expressed their alarm over the conflict he had created. They feared it would spark persecution against them by the Philistines. The men of Judah also revealed their ungodliness in their failure to recognize that

---

[16]Cundall and Morris, *Judges and Ruth*, p. 170.

God had raised up Samson to be a judge who would deliver them from the power of the Philistines. They should have supported Samson in his role of delivering their fellow Israelites; instead, they reminded, "Don't you realize that the Philistines are rulers over us?" (15:11).

Samson made them promise to not attack him. This request was not out of fear but rather out of consideration for them. If they had fallen on him, he would have protected himself, slaughtering many men of Judah. Samson lived by the law in at least the areas that suited him (Deut. 19:21)! Having received their promise, Samson permitted them to bind him with two new ropes.

2) *Samson slaughters the Philistines* (15:14–17). As the men of Judah brought Samson to the Philistines, a great shout went up from their camp: they were about to receive their nemesis as a captive! Shouting was common in a confrontation with the enemy (Josh. 6:16; Judg. 7:20; 1 Sam. 17:20, 52). However, the Philistines joy was to be short-lived, for Israel's judge was about to inflict severe punishment on them. When the Spirit of the Lord came upon Samson in power (14:6, 19), he broke the ropes as easily as though they were pieces of burned flax; the ropes were totally incapable of holding him and dropped from his arms as though they had turned to ashes.

Samson picked up the fresh jawbone of a donkey, pursued the Philistines, and killed a thousand of them. A fresh jawbone was essential since an old one would have been brittle and would have broken quickly.

No mention is made here of the role of the men of Judah. Did they support Samson? From the silence it is reasonable to conclude they did not. The Israelites evidently placed themselves under Philistine rule with a resolute subjection, lacking sensitivity to God's leading and lacking faith that He would deliver them from the Philistine oppression. For Samson, however, it was a great victory as he slew one thousand Philistines.

Samson concluded this extraordinary episode by composing a poem (15:16). Hebrew poetry emphasizes meter and balance of thought rather than rhyme as in English poetry. In Samson's poem there is a play on the words donkey and heap, both being *hamor* in Hebrew. The grammatical device used is called antanaclasis—the repetition of the same word in the same sentence but with different meanings. Thus the poem may be rendered:

> With the jaw-bone of an ass (*hamor*),
> A mass (*hamor*), yea, masses;
> With the jaw-bone of an ass,
> I slew a thousand men.[17]

The second line, translated "I have made donkeys of them," literally is "heap, heaps" and may indicate the manner in which Samson slew the Philistines. It appears Samson pursued and killed a number of Philistines, piled them in a heap, pursued and killed another group, and also piled them in a heap. The poem thus suggests several encounters rather than one battle.

When Samson's conquest of the Philistines was completed, he threw away the jawbone and named the scene of the battle Ramath Lehi ("jawbone height"). The earlier designation Lehi (15:9) was used proleptically in anticipation of Samson's conquest and naming of the place.

3) *Samson assuaged by God* (15:18–20). The following episode demonstrates once more that Samson functioned largely according to his viscerogenic desires. First, he was attracted to a Philistine woman because she was beautiful; second, he impulsively ate honey from the carcass of a loin; now he demanded water from God to quench his thirst. Samson was hot and thirsty because this was the time of the wheat harvest (15:1); he had pursued the Philistines in the heat of summer. Samson cried to the Lord in an "impudent harangue,"[18] revealing an attitude not unlike that of the complaining Israelites when they tested God in the desert (Exod. 17:1–7). Yet it is interesting to note that Samson saw himself as the Lord's "servant" (Hebrew, *ebed*), a term normally used in a polite form of address to God (15:18; cf. Exod. 4:10; Num. 11:11; 1 Sam. 3:9, 10; 25:39 et al.).[19] The statement indicates that Samson understood his unique calling.

In response to Samson's appeal God opened up the hollow place (literally, mortar), a depression in a rock from which flowed spring water. Samson drank some water and his strength returned (15:19). As a result he named the spring En Hakkore ("the spring of the caller").

Verse 20 is a summary statement indicating that Samson led Israel for twenty years as judge. If the previously suggested date of 1075–1055 B.C. is generally correct, it is possible that the battle of Aphek took place during the ministry of Samson, in this conflict Israel was defeated

---

[17]E. W. Bullinger, *Figures of Speech Used in the Bible* (Grand Rapids: Baker, 1968 reprint), p. 288.

[18]Boling, *Judges*, AB, p. 239.

[19]Brown, Driver, and Briggs, *Hebrew and English Lexicon*, p. 714.

by the Philistines, who captured the ark (1 Sam. 4:1ff.).

c) *Gazite gate destroyed* (16:1–3)

The narration of Samson's exploits continues, indicating particularly his weakness for women. This fault was destined to ultimately be his undoing.

One day Samson went down to Gaza, a city of the Philistines south of Ashkelon and three miles inland from the Mediterranean Sea. Gaza lay on the trade and military route to Egypt. Although Joshua had initially conquered Gaza (Josh. 10:41), the city remained a Philistine stronghold (Josh. 11:22; 13:3; Judg. 1:18–19).

Samson apparently saw no discrepancy about being the servant of the Lord and yet spending the night with a prostitute! The life of Samson remains one of the great tragedies of biblical history in view of what he might have been if he had obeyed God. The fundamental principles by which God dealt with Israel—obedience brings blessing; disobedience brings chastisement (Deut. 28)—would ultimately have a negative effect in Samson's life.

When the people of Gaza heard that Samson was in the walled city, they lay in wait for him at the city gate. They knew he would have to exit through the same gate by which he entered. They saw no need to search the city for him at night; rather, they chose to wait until morning when he would be leaving and to apprehend him then. However, Samson surprised them by leaving in the middle of the night; as he left he used his great strength to tear the gate posts out of the ground and to walk off with the entire gate structure, including the posts and the bar! That this was a miracle is evident from the average size and construction of a city gate. It was usually in two halves, constructed of wood, and covered with metal. "The width of the principal gate was about thirteen or fourteen feet."[20] Samson put the gate on his shoulders and carried it to Hebron, forty miles distant and uphill![21]

4. *Deception and death of Samson* (16:4–31a)

The narrative records the final stage of Samson's life as he met his match in Delilah. After she continued to pressure Samson, he finally revealed the source of his strength.

a) *Deception of Delilah* (16:4–22)

[20]S. Barabas, "Gate," ZPEB, 2:656.
[21]Leon Wood states, "The words, 'before Hebron' are used in connection with this hill. The translation 'before' is of the Hebrew *'al-pene*, which need not mean that this hill itself was near Hebron, but only in the direction of Hebron," *Distressing Days*, p. 339.

1) *Instigation of the Philistines* (16:4–5). Samson's attention soon turned to another Philistine woman, Delilah, who lived in the Valley of Sorek, identified as Wadi es Sarar, beginning about fifteen miles southwest of Jerusalem and running westward through the Shephelah to the Mediterranean Sea. The name Delilah means flirtatious or devotee. If the latter, then her name is linked to the fertility-goddess, Ishtar.[22]

The rulers of the five Philistine cities recognized Samson as their nemesis, and when they realized Samson had an interest in Delilah, they planned a trap for him in an effort to discover the secret of his strength. "The Philistine princes thought that Samson's supernatural strength arose from something external, which he wore or carried about with him as an amulet."[23] Should Delilah discover the secret to Samson's strength, the Philistine rulers promised to each pay her eleven hundred shekels of silver. The number emphasizes that Delilah would receive a full thousand from each ruler. Although there was no consistent weight for a shekel, the average shekel weighed between .401 and .408 ounces; hence eleven hundred shekels weighed approximately twenty-eight pounds.

2) *First attempt* (16:6–9). Delilah plied Samson for the secret of his strength and how he could be tied so that he could be subdued. He responded that if he were tied with seven fresh thongs, he would become as weak as any other man. The term thongs or bowstrings refers to twisted animal intestines, while the emphasis that they should be fresh suggests their supple quality in being tied into knots that would not be possible if they were dry. Seven as used in Scripture suggests thoroughness or completeness.

The Philistine rulers brought Delilah seven fresh thongs, and Delilah used these to bind Samson (16:8). While the Philistines remained hidden in the room, Delilah called, "Samson, the Philistines are upon you!" (v. 9). It is apparent that the Philistines remained hidden to see whether Samson could indeed be bound. Each time that Samson freed himself the Philistines remained hidden so that Samson did not discover their presence. Had he been aware of the Philistines' presence and Delilah's plot, it is conceivable he would not have divulged his secret to Delilah. When Delilah called her warning to Samson, he snapped the sinews as easily as one would break a piece of string that is exposed to a flame.

[22]Gray, *Joshua, Judges and Ruth*, CB, p. 357.
[23]Keil and Delitzsch, *Joshua, Judges, Ruth*, p. 419.

3) *Second attempt* (16:10–12). No doubt some time lapsed between these events, for the Philistines would need time to procure the materials Delilah requested for tying Samson.

Delilah was upset when she discovered Samson was teasing her and had not told the truth. Once more she asked Samson to tell her how he could be bound so that he could not escape. This time Samson told her that if he would be bound with new ropes, he would become weak as any other man (16:11). Unknown to Delilah, new ropes had already been tried on Samson by the men of Judah (15:13). When Delilah bound Samson with the new ropes and playfully called out, "Samson, the Philistines are upon you!" he snapped the ropes as though they were threads. Meanwhile, the Philistines remained hidden in the room.

4) *Third attempt* (16:13–14). Samson's resistance seemed to be weakening as he told her the answer was in connection with his hair. Perhaps this was a clue that he, under continued pressure, eventually would divulge his secret.

As Delilah again implored Samson to tell her his secret, he explained that if she would weave the seven locks of his hair into the weaving material of the loom so that his hair became a part of the woven material, he would be as weak as any other man.[24] When Delilah again warned Samson of the approach of the Philistines, he pulled out the pin and his hair that had been woven into the fabric.

5) *Confession of Samson* (16:15–17). Delilah now became more persistent than ever. She was upset that Samson had deceived her three times and reminded him of his deceitfulness. She indicated that if he genuinely loved her, he would not withhold secrets from her. She, of course, didn't love Samson but was interested in the wealth that his capture would bring her. Delilah began "nagging" Samson daily until he became "tired to death" (16:16). *Soq*, the Hebrew word for "nagging" in verse 16, is translated "press" in 14:17 (where it yielded results for Samson's wife). *Soq* means to bring pressure or distress. The term is used in Isaiah 29:2 of an army encircling Jerusalem to bring pressure and distress on the city. Delilah pressured Samson daily until he succumbed to her nagging.

---

[24]There is a textual problem in verses 13–14. The Hebrew Massoretic Text omits "'and tighten it with the pin, I'll become as weak as any other man.' So while he was sleeping, Delilah took the seven braids of his head, wove them into the fabric," evidently through haplography. The Septuagint supplies the complete, original statement.

Samson finally betrayed his secret, telling Delilah of his Nazirite vow. He explained that should his hair be cut, he would lose his strength.

6) *Affliction of Samson* (16:18–22). It appears the Philistines had lost hope that Delilah would discover the truth about Samson, for they departed from her home. After Delilah convinced them that she had discovered Samson's secret they returned and brought the money with them that they had agreed to pay her.

As Samson slept on Delilah's lap, presumably as before, Delilah had a man shave the seven braids of his hair. Samson's strength was now gone. As long as Samson's hair remained uncut, he maintained proof that he was a Nazirite; when he allowed his hair to be cut, he indicated his repudiation of the Nazirite vow. When Delilah called out as previously, Samson thought he could free himself as before; "But he did not know that the LORD had left him" (16:20). Samson's uncut hair had reflected his separation to the Lord as well as his obedience to the vow. When Samson disobeyed, the strength from the Lord left him.

Recognizing that Samson's strength was gone, the Philistines quickly came out of hiding and captured him. They gouged out his eyes, perhaps following the Persian practice of digging them out with red hot needles. It may be significant that the Philistines brought Samson down to Gaza since that was the site of an earlier conquest of Samson (16:1–3). The place where Samson had enjoyed a conquest would now be the place where he would be ridiculed. Samson was bound at Gaza with bronze shackles and put to work grinding in the prison. Both Samson's hands and feet were shackled as he performed this humiliating work normally carried out by women or slaves (Exod. 11:5; Isa. 47:2). Greeks and Romans sentenced their slaves and occasionally free people to this hard and humiliating labor.

While Samson was in prison, his hair began to grow (16:22). The statement anticipates the impending climax when Samson's strength would ultimately return. The strength, however, was not in his hair.

> Samson was strong because he was dedicated to God, as long as he preserved the signs of his dedication. But as soon as he lost those signs, he fell into the utmost weakness in consequence. The whole of Samson's misfortune came upon him, therefore, because he attributed to himself some portion of what God did through him. God permitted him to lose his strength, that he might learn by experience how utterly powerless he was without the help of God.[25]

---

[25]Keil and Delitzsch, *Joshua, Judges, Ruth*, p. 423.

b) *Death of Samson* (16:23–31a)

1) *Display of Samson* (16:23–27). These verses describe why Samson would ultimately have to be vindicated—because shame had been brought on the name of the Lord through the humiliation of Samson amid the worship of Dagon. Ultimately, the Lord's name had to be vindicated.

The Philistines attributed their capture of Samson to Dagon, their god, and assembled to offer a sacrifice to their god. An earlier view was that Dagon was a fish-god; however, that view is not as commonly held today. It is generally believed now that Dagon was a grain-god since Dagon means grain. Another view is that Dagon was a Mesopotamian storm-god, a concept related to grain through rain that produced the crops of grain. Dagon was introduced to Canaan through the migration in the early second millennium and received a prominent place in the Canaanite pantheon.[26]

When the Philistines were in high spirits, they called for Samson to entertain them. The expression "in high spirits" is frequently associated with drinking or drunkenness (cf. 1 Sam. 25:36; 2 Sam. 13:28). In their drunken celebration and praise of Dagon, the Philistines called for Samson to entertain them. The verb "to entertain" (Hebrew, *sahaq*) may mean "to laugh at, usually in contempt, derision."[27] They were intent on making Samson a public spectacle as he entertained them.

A young lad led Samson out into the courtyard and assisted him to his position between the support pillars of the temple. Several temples have been discovered that provide information concerning the nature of the temple at Gaza. The spectators were seated on a roof that extended out into the courtyard. The roof was supported by wooden columns placed on stone bases. The central columns supporting the roof were close together, enabling Samson to reach both of them. The narrative emphasizes that a large audience had gathered in anticipation of the event to follow; three thousand men and women were on the roof watching Samson perform (16:27).

2) *Destruction of the Philistines* (16:28–30). The final feat of Samson should not be attributed to the return of his hair as much as to his repentant attitude and prayer (16:28). It seems that the humiliation he

---

[26]Bruce K. Waltke, "דָּגָן" *Theological Wordbook*, vol. 1, p. 183; Helmer Ringgren, "דָּגָן" pp. 139–42.

[27]Brown, Driver, and Briggs, *Hebrew and English Lexicon*, p. 965.

suffered at the hands of the Philistines was the instrument God used in bringing him to repentance. It is evident from the statement in verse 28 that the loss of Samson's eyes remained a grievous experience for him. The solemnity of the prayer is seen in Samson's use of three different names for God in his appeal. The title "Sovereign" (Hebrew, *Adonai*) refers to God as the almighty Ruler who rules over all and before whom all are subject. Although Samson was a captive of the Philistines, the Lord ruled sovereignly over them all. The name "LORD" is derived from the verb "to be" (cf. Exod. 3:14–15) and refers to God as the eternally unchanging and ever-existing One. The name is sometimes translated Yahweh and refers to God in His covenant relationship with Israel (Exod. 6:2–3). The name "God" is Elohim and comes from a root word meaning strong and denoting God as the strong One and the object of fear.

Samson did not request strength to commit suicide but to avenge the loss of his eyes. As the Lord's servant he desired to vindicate the name of the Lord in his final role as a judge of Israel and leader against Israel's enemies, the Philistines. Samson's request was for God to strengthen him in a final act against the enemy in which a devastating blow would be inflicted against the idolatrous Philistines. Recognizing he would die with the Philistines, he appealed for a victory over them (16:30). Then he pushed the support columns with all his might and the structure collapsed, killing not only the people on the roof (v. 27), but also many dignitaries and people on whom the roof fell. Samson's prayer was answered in such a way that his final act of vengeance resulted in the death of more Philistines than he had killed during his life.

3) *Death of Samson* (16:31a). Samson's brothers and family came, removed the body from the ruins, and buried it in the family plot between Zorah and Eshtaol. The fact that this was possible indicates the Philistines offered no resistance—they were in a state of confusion and bewilderment through the carnage wrought by Samson.

D. Silence: twenty years (16:31b)

Samson's unique service for Israel neutralized the effectiveness of the Philistines for twenty years.

For Further Study

1. Carefully study the life of Samson. Why did he fail? Analyze his weaknesses and causes for failure.

2. Read an article on Samson in a Bible dictionary or encyclopedia.

3. What positive and negative lessons can you learn from the life of Samson?

4. Read an article on the Philistines in a Bible dictionary or encyclopedia.

PART THREE:

CONSEQUENCES OF THE PERIOD OF THE JUDGES

Chapter 9

Idolatry
(Judges 17:1–18:31)

The death of Samson brings the chronological section of the period of the judges to an end; in fact, Samson served as a judge during the early life of Samuel the prophet. Chapter 17–21 deal with the general conditions that existed during the times of the judges, a major theme being "in those days Israel had no king; everyone did as he saw fit" (17:6; 18:1; 19:1; 21:25). This period also illustrates the lack of national leadership in Israel, for no single judge was able to provide direction for all the people. Through this failure the period of the kings of Israel is anticipated; it would not be many years hence when the people would demand a king (1 Sam. 8:1ff.).

A. Idolatry of Micah (17:1–13)

1. *Micah and his idols* (17:1–6)

The appendix of Judges introduces Micah, who was from the hill country of Ephraim. The name Micah ("who is like Yahweh?") probably typifies the religious syncretism that was common in that day in which the Israelites combined the worship of the Lord with the worship of idols.[1] A major step in the rapid decline of the northern kingdom took place when Jeroboam I established syncretistic worship by making both Dan and Bethel major worship centers so that his people would not have to worship at Jerusalem (1 Kings 12:28–29).

A commentary on the times is seen in the apostasy of the Ephraim-

---

[1]For an important discussion on the religion of Israel and her neighbors, see William F. Albright, *Archaeology and the Religion of Israel* (Baltimore: The Johns Hopkins Press, 1956) and William F. Albright, *Yahweh and the Gods of Canaan* (New York: Doubleday, 1968).

ites despite the fact that the tabernacle was situated at Shiloh in their
tribal territory at this time (1 Sam. 1:3).

Micah had stolen eleven hundred shekels of silver from his mother
but then heard her "curse" (Hebrew, *alah*) on the thief (17:2). The
curse was a conditional imprecation to protect a person's property. It
was made publicly and considered to be in effect when the thief or the
one finding the article failed to return it to the owner. The curse was
similar to the declaration of the Bedouin, who upon losing something
declares, "I hold the person who finds this thing responsible for it. If he
keeps it, may Allah cut off his property and his family from him."[2]

Having heard the curse, Micah became frightened to the extent that
he refused to use the silver and instead gave it back to his mother, who
blessed him in return. The blessing may have been an act to counteract
the curse that had been on her son. Since the silver was returned to
her, she consecrated it to the Lord by fashioning an idol!

When Micah returned the silver to his mother, she weighed out two
hundred shekels and gave this amount to a silversmith to fashion an
"image" and an "idol" (17:4). Since all the silver was dedicated to the
Lord and could not be used for profane purposes, it is noteworthy that
only two hundred shekels were set apart. She may have kept back
some silver as did Ananias and Sapphira (Acts 5:1–11), or she used the
remainder in some other religious endeavor. It is not entirely clear
from the text whether there were two images or one. The term image
refers to an idolatrous image of wood or metal while idol refers to
something cast or poured. The most suitable conclusion is that the
image refers to the idolatrous form itself, while the idol has reference
to the foundation or base on which the idol stood. The image may well
have been a calf that was to represent the Lord.[3] When completed the
image was placed in the house of Micah (17:4).

Micah's house was now termed a "shrine" (17:5; literally "a house of
God") because his house harbored an idol and was considered a minia-
ture temple. The people would come to his house to determine the will
of God. Micah also established his own priesthood when he consecrated his sons as priests since under the Mosaic system only descendants of the tribe of Levi could serve as priests (Num. 3–4). As an
Ephraimite Micah and his family were disqualified from the Mosaic
priesthood. The ephod that Micah made for his son recalled the vest

---

[2]Josef Scharbert, "אָלָה," *Theological Dictionary*, pp. 261–66.
[3]Keil and Delitzsch, *Joshua, Judges, Ruth*, p. 430.

worn by the Levitical high priest (Exod. 28:6–14). In addition, Micah
had household idols (teraphim) that were household gods worshiped
"as the givers of earthly prosperity."[4]

The summary statement in verse 6 testifies to the chaotic moral
conditions that were prevalent in Israel at this time. There was no
unifying leader like Moses or Joshua to lead the nation in obedience to
God through the Mosaic covenant; rather, "everyone did as he saw fit"
(21:25).

2. Micah and his priest (17:7–13)

This story is important in noting further the degradation of the
period of the judges. Verses 1–6 show the apostasy of the people into
idolatry; verses 7–13 show the apostasy of the priests.

A young Levite who had been temporarily living as an alien in
Bethlehem left Judah to find a place of service where he would receive
support. As a Levite he was not of the family of Judah, but he may have
been native to the territory of Judah since the Levites were scattered
throughout the land of Israel. The Lord had designated forty-eight
cities throughout the land as places of residence for the priests and
Levites to minister to the nation (Josh. 21). However, Bethlehem was
not one of those cities, and the Levite's presence outside one of the
forty-eight cities may also reflect the existing chaotic conditions. Furthermore, the cities of Judah were designated for the Kohathites, the
priestly descendants of Levi, rather than the Gershonites or Merarites
who were of the Levitical tribe but not priests. This may further indicate that Judah was not the Levite's native home.

Having departed from Bethlehem in Judah (so designated to distinguish it from Bethlehem in Zebulun as in Joshua 19:15), the Levite had
come to Micah's house in the hill country of Ephraim (17:8). When the
Levite informed Micah that he was looking for a place to stay, Micah
invited the man to be his "father and priest" (17:10). "Father," a title of
honor and respect, was sometimes conferred on a prophet, priest, or
friend to denote his authority in spiritual counsel (Gen. 45:8; 2 Kings
2:12; 6:21; 13:14). When Micah offered the man an annual salary of ten
shekels of silver, shelter, and clothing, the Levite accepted; apparently
he considered the offer advantageous. The ten-shekel payment is interesting in the light of the amount of silver available in Micah's home
(17:2).

---

[4]Keil and Delitzsch, Joshua, Judges, Ruth, p. 430.

Micah "installed" the Levite as priest in his home and the young man lived there (17:12). The expression "installed" in the literal Hebrew reads "filled the hand"; elsewhere the idiom refers to the ordination ritual in which the priest literally received in his hand portion of the sacrifice (Exod. 28:41; 29:9; cf. vv. 31–34).

This incident (17:13) demonstrates that superstition prevailed in Israel at that time. The people recognized that the Levites were the priestly tribe; if a man was able to have his own Levite, he could certainly expect God's blessing on his life! Although Micah was amply supplied with the externals of religion—his own son as priest, a Levite as his personal priest, an expensive idol, and additional household idols—there is no mention of faith, a necessary element of true faith.

B. Idolatry of Dan (18:1–31)

The relationship of chapters 17 and 18 is evident: chapter 17 emphasizes the apostasy of individuals while chapter 18 takes note of the apostasy of a tribe. All these events underscore the theme "In those days Israel had no king; everyone did as he saw fit" (21:25).

1. *Danites seek new territory* (18:1–6)

The tribe of Dan was eventually split in two, with one group remaining in the central area and another group going north. The problem of the Danites is seen in 1:34–36 where they were unable to completely occupy the territory that had been allotted to them. The Amorites remained lodged in Danite territory and prevented them from occupying their allotment (Josh. 19:41–46). The northern migration (but not the reason for it) is also recorded in Joshua 19:47–48.

In preparation for the migration, the Danites sent five warriors to explore the northern territory, reminiscent of Numbers 13 where twelve men went forth to spy out the promised Land from the Israelite camp at Kadesh Barnea. The warriors were from Zorah and Eshtaol, the territory of Samson. While no time indicator is given, it appears this incident took place prior to Samson's ministry.

On their way north the Danites passed through Ephraim and came to Micah's home where they spent the night. As they approached the house they recognized the voice of the Levite (18:3). It is uncertain whether they recognized the voice of the Levite as an individual, or whether they recognized his accent and thus identified him as from Judah. In response to their inquiry, the Levite informed them that

Micah had hired him as his priest (v. 4). The Levite's answer prompted the Danites to have the Levite inquire of God whether or not they would prosper in their venture. The request was ironic, for such an inquiry ought to have been made before they left on their expedition! The Levite answered, "Go in peace. Your journey has the LORD'S approval" (v. 6). He may have simply responded to their request without consulting the oracle. In any case the response was a reassurance, for the Levite was reminding them that their journey was "in front of the LORD" (literal Hebrew), that is, under His watchful eye (cf. 1 Sam. 1:17; 1 Kings 22:6 for similar statements).

2. Danites suggest northern migration (18:7–13)

The five warriors came to Laish, north of Hazor and Lake Huleh at one of the sources of the Jordan River. The city formerly was known as Leshem (Josh. 19:47) but the name was changed to Dan. The location came to symbolize the northern extremity of the nation even as Beersheba denoted the southern extremity (20:1).

The Danites discovered the inhabitants "were living in safety, like the Sidonians, unsuspecting and secure" (18:7). The statement that the people of Laish lived in safety may suggest that they lived without defenses since excavations have revealed the city was unwalled.[5] Their linkage with the Sidonians further stresses their peaceful estate since the Sidonians concentrated on trade and commerce rather than war. In addition, Laish was secure in its isolation, being protected on the north by Mount Hermon and shielded from the Phoenicians on the northwest by the Lebanon range.

The middle of verse 7 contains a textual problem, with the NIV reading, "And since their land lacked nothing, they were prosperous," whereas the NASB says, "for there was no ruler humiliating them for anything in the land." The NASB translation seems to shed particular light on the situation since Laish was sufficiently isolated that no foreign ruler had subjugated the city.

When the Danite spies returned to Zorah and Eshtaol, they brought their optimistic report: "Come on, let's attack them!" (18:9; cf. Num. 13:25–33 where the ten spies gave their faithless report). The enthusiastic warriors were impatient and determined to capture Laish immediately; hence they provoked their brothers to immediate action.

---

[5]Boling, *Judges*, AB, p. 263.

The Danite warriors depicted the people of Laish as living in a careless security; the conquest would be easy! Moreover, God had put this new territory into their hands—no doubt a reference to the blessing of Micah's priest (18:6).

In response to the report six hundred fighting men along with women and children set out for Laish. The number is surprisingly low since the Danites numbered 64,400 in the new census immediately prior to the conquest of the land (Num. 26:42–43). It is possible that the Danite population had been reduced by their enemies; more plausible, however, is the suggestion that the majority decided to remain in their native territory.

The Danites journeyed less than ten miles on the first day of their trip, camping west of Kiriath Jearim in Judah (18:12) and naming the site Mahaneh Dan ("Dan's camp"). From there they advanced to Micah's house in the hill country of Ephraim.

3. Danites steal Micah's idols (18:14–20)

As the Danites came to the vicinity of Micah's house, the five men who had spied out the territory remembered Micah and his household idols. The men's advice, "Now you know what to do" (18:14) suggests that their fellow Danites should not fail in the opportunity to procure their own gods and establish their own worship. The five men may have been encouraged by their earlier success (v. 6). The quintet came to Micah's house and "greeted him" (literally, they asked him concerning his health), which was the customary greeting (cf. Exod. 18:7). To discourage resistance the six hundred men stationed themselves at the entrance to the gate (18:16). This would normally refer to the entrance to a town, but here it probably refers to the doorway to Micah's carved image, ephod, household gods, and cast idol, while the priest stood with the six hundred armed men at the entrance. When the priest protested the Danites warned him, "Don't say a word" (18:19; literally, "put your hand over your mouth," which is a Hebrew idiom emphasizing silence, Job 21:5; 29:9; 40:4; Prov. 30:32). Then in a manner reminiscent of Micah (17:10), they invited the priest to be their father and priest (18:19). In order to lure the priest they said it would be much better for him to serve a tribe and a clan than only one man's household. The priest was an opportunist and did not need further persuasion; he left Micah and joined the Danites. Having made this decision, the priest apparently regained custody of the household gods.

4. Danites suppress Micah (18:21–26)

As the Danites left Micah's home they put the women and children as well as their valuables in front of them for fear of being attacked from the rear by Micah and his people. Micah assembled his neighbors to help him pursue the Danites and retrieve his gods (what a dilemma—having to pursue thieves who have stolen one's gods!). The neighbors would have had more than a casual interest in the event since they would have consulted the priest and his idols in their worship.

As Micah and his neighbors drew near, they cried out to the Danites, who expressed their annoyance at having been pursued. Micah revealed his extreme frustration in his response (18:24). They had taken his gods and his priest; he had nothing left. The Danites reminded Micah of the grave danger in resisting them; should he argue with them, some "hot-tempered" (literally, "bitter of soul," denoting someone fierce as a bear that has been robbed of her cubs, cf. 2 Sam. 17:8) men would attack and kill the whole family.

Having threatened Micah and his men, the Danites resumed their journey (18:26). Assessing his strength, Micah realized that he and his friends were no match for the six hundred armed Danites; therefore he turned his men around and started back home. The incident once more bears witness to the depravity of the days of the judges.

5. Danites seize new territory (18:27–29)

The Danites continued on to Laish with the Levite and the idols Micah had made. The narrative continues to emphasize the helplessness of the peaceful city. The Danites attacked, killed the inhabitants, and burned the city. Possibly the Danites thought Deuteronomy 7:2 justified their action and hence dealt with Laish in the same manner that Israel had dealt with Jericho in Joshua's day (Josh. 6:24). The Sidonians were not able to help Laish, nor was anyone else since the city had no defense treaty with any other nation. Laish was isolated in a valley near Beth Rehob ("house of the open place"), probably to be identified with the northern extremity of the spies' mission (Num. 13:21). This territory was occupied by the Arameans during the beginning of David's reign (2 Sam. 10:6). The Danites rebuilt Laish and renamed the city Dan after their tribal ancestor, who was born of Rachel's servant, Bilhah (Gen. 30:6).

6. *Danites set up idolatrous worship* (18:30-31)

In the city the Danites set up the idol (the text is singular) and established a false worship center. Jeroboam I later set up a golden calf at Dan, thus contributing to the demise of the northern kingdom (1 Kings 12:28-29). The Danites also established Jonathan, the son of Gershom, the son of Moses, as priest. It is generally conceded that Jonathan is the name of the Levite (17:7). There is a textual problem as the Massoretic Text reads "son of Manasseh." However, some other manuscripts have "sons of Moses," which is probably correct inasmuch as the Massoretes were determined to disassociate Moses from idolatry.

The rival priesthood continued "until the time of the captivity of the land" (18:30). The reference may be to the conquest and captivity of Syria and the northern territory of Israel by Tiglath-Pileser III in 732 B.C., or to the fall of the northern kingdom to Shalmaneser V in 722 B.C. (2 Kings 15:29; 17:1-6).

For Further Study

1. Read an article on idolatry in a Bible dictionary or encyclopedia.

2. Can idolatry exist without an outward image? In what forms could idolatry exist today?

3. Distinguish between religion, superstition, and a true faith as seen in chapters 17-18.

4. Show how one sin leads to another in the history of the Danites.

Chapter 10

Immorality
(Judges 19:1–30)

This chapter further develops the apostasy during the time of the judges. It traces the moral depravity of the religious leaders, with the corruption spreading to the entire nation. It reflects a departure from the morals and standards of the Mosaic covenant. The mention of Phinehas, Eleazar's son (20:28), suggests that the events of chapters 19–21 took place early in Israel's history, perhaps soon after the death of Joshua.

A. Disruption between the Levite and the concubine (19:1–15)

1. *Separation* (19:1–2)

The reader is reminded that the ensuing immoral event took place in the days when Israel had no human king, although God was their King in the theocracy (1 Sam. 8:7). This Levite, like the Levite of chapters 17–18, was living temporarily in the remote area of the hill country of Ephraim instead of in a Levitical city. This may once more indicate the failure of the Levites to fulfill their God-ordained task of instructing the nation in the law of God. This Levite had taken a concubine for himself from Bethlehem in Judah. A concubine was considered a wife, although of secondary status, as is indicated by the use of words expressing the following relationships: "husband" (19:3), "father-in-law" (v. 4), and "son-in-law" (v. 5). She was not merely a mistress and did not live with a man as an unmarried woman. Concubinage was an outgrowth of polygamy. Concubines were usually a sign of wealth and status in the Old Testament (Esth. 2:14; Song of Songs 6:8; Dan. 5:3, 23).[1]

---

[1] Victor P. Hamilton, "פִּלֶגֶשׁ," *Theological Wordbook*, vol. 2, p. 724.

The Levite's concubine left him and went back to her father's house in Bethlehem. The Massoretic Text indicates she was "unfaithful" (19:2; "played the harlot," NASB), while some Septuagint manuscripts and Old Latin versions read "became angry with him." If the former is the true reading, the law required the death penalty for adultery (Lev. 20:10).

2. Reconciliation (19:3-4)

In order to effect a reconciliation the Levite journeyed to his father-in-law's home after the concubine had been absent four months. He went "to persuade her to return" (19:3; literally, "to speak to her heart," cf. Gen. 34:3). Apparently he was successful since she brought him into her father's house (19:3). Hopeful of a reconciliation, the Levite had brought two donkeys for the return trip, although according to Eastern custom the woman would normally walk. The unusual joy of the father in seeing his son-in-law may indicate the apologetic nature of his hospitality and his desire for the reconciliation.

3. Supplication (19:5-9)

Leisureliness is typical of an Eastern setting. Having remained in his father-in-law's home for three days, the Levite rose early on the fourth day and prepared to depart. But the girl's father coaxed the Levite to refresh himself with some bread (cf. Gen. 18:5) before leaving. When the evening approached, the girl's father persuaded him to remain for the night (19:7). The Levite rose to go early in the morning of the fifth day but was once more delayed by the man's hospitality and suggestion that he wait until "afternoon" (19:8; literally, "until the day declines"; the phrase is an idiom used by modern Arab peasants in referring to any time after 3:00 P.M.[2]). When the Levite was determined to leave, the man pressured him to remain until the following morning. He reminded the Levite, "It's almost evening" (19:9).

4. Reception (19:10-15)

On the evening of the fifth day the Levite insisted on returning home and took his concubine and departed. Traveling north they came to the city of Jebus, about six miles from Bethlehem, a journey of about two hours. The city was named Jebus ("to be trampled down") after the Jebusites, a non-Hebrew people who remained in possession of the city

---

[2]Gray, *Joshua, Judges and Ruth*, CB, p. 374.

until the conquest by David (see discussion at 1:7–8, 21). Not wishing
to spend the night in a city of foreigners, the Levite resisted the
suggestion of his servant and determined to reach either Gibeah or
Ramah. As the sun set they approached Gibeah in the territory of
Benjamin, about two miles north of Jerusalem. Gibeah ("hill"), modern
Tell el Ful, was excavated by William F. Albright beginning in 1922.
The city was strategically located, being on a hill rising to 2840 feet
above sea level and situated along the main road running north of
Jerusalem. It was originally an unfortified village, but later Saul built a
fortress on the site.[3]

The travelers entered Gibeah and "sat in the city square, but no one
took them into his home for the night" (19:15). The city square was a
public gathering place just inside the entrance to the city. Here busi-
ness transactions took place, merchants sold wares, legal matters were
settled, and people visited friends (Gen. 19:1; 34:20; 2 Sam. 15:2). The
neglect of the travelers is a further indictment of the period since
hospitality was a common custom and courtesy accorded to strangers in
the East.

B. Display of hospitality (19:16–21)

As the three rested in the city square, an old man who had been
working in the fields approached. While questioning them concerning
their journey, he discovered they were from the hill country of Ephraim. Since the old man was also a native of Ephraim, he invited them
to spend the night at his house. The Levite replied, "I am going to the
house of the LORD" (19:18). The Levite's statement is not exactly clear;
perhaps it should be rendered, "I am now going to my house" (NASB)
according to the Septuagint. Cassel understands the statement as denoting the Levite's vocation, not his destination:

> He expresses this paraphrastically, by saying that "he walks in the house
> of God," namely, as a servant of God. He chooses this form of expression
> in order to invite hospitality, and to place the refusal of it in its worst
> light. A man who is at home in the House of God, no one here receives
> into his house.[4]

The Levite reminded the old Ephraimite that he had sufficient fodder for the donkeys and food for the three of them, but at the old man's

[3]Garstang, *Joshua Judges*, pp. 160, 378–79; Charles F. Pfeiffer, ed., *The Biblical
World* (Grand Rapids: Baker, 1966), pp. 259–61.
[4]Cassel, "The Book of Judges," *Lange's*, p. 244.

insistence the Levite received his hospitality. The display of hospitality is seen in the statement "You are welcome at my house" (19:20; literally, "Peace to you," NASB). It was a reminder that they would find peace in his home (cf. Luke 10:5ff.). When they came to the man's home he provided fodder for the donkeys, water to wash their feet, and food. This display of hospitality was common (cf. Gen. 18:4–5; 19:2; 24:25, 32).

C. Depravity of the Benjamites (19:22–26)

The hospitality was interrupted by the demands of a group of "wicked men" (19:22; literally, "sons of Belial"; Hebrew, *beliyya'al*).[5] The origin of the term is unclear. Some suggest it had its origin in the name Baal; others suggest it comes from the word meaning yoke and thus refers to those who throw off the yoke of God; still others suggest it comes from a root word meaning to entangle or confuse, or to harm or injure. The use of the Hebrew term *beliyya'al* sheds light on the meaning since it is found in juridical contexts. Since order in society is dependent on maintenance of the law, lawbreakers are called sons of *beliyya'al*. This basic meaning has a variety of applications where the Hebrew term occurs; it is used of the idolatrous ("wicked," Deut. 13:13); of those who neglect responsibility to the poor ("wicked," Deut. 15:9); of homosexuals ("wicked," Judg. 19:22; 20:13); of drunkards ("wicked," 1 Sam. 1:16); of the immoral and rebellious ("wicked," 1 Sam. 2:12); or those who rebel against the government ("troublemakers," 1 Sam. 10:27; "troublemaker," 2 Sam. 20:1); and of those who mock at social justice ("corrupt," Prov. 19:28).

The wicked men surrounded the house, pounded on the door, and shouted at the man, "Bring out the man who came to your house so we can have sex with him" (19:22). The latter clause in Hebrew reads literally "that we may know him," a euphemism for sexual intercourse that occurs frequently in the Hebrew Bible (cf. Gen. 4:1, 17, 25; 24:16; 38:26 et al.); here it denotes a homosexual relationship. The man protested since he as the host was responsible for the welfare and well-being of his guests. *Nebala*, the Hebrew word translated "disgraceful thing" (19:23) and "wicked thing" elsewhere, is frequently used of offenses against the laws governing the relations of the sexes (Gen. 34:7; 2 Sam. 13:12; Deut. 22:21).[6]

---

[5]Benedikt Otzen, "בְּלִיַּעַל," *Theological Dictionary*, vol. 2, pp. 131–36.
[6]Moore, *Judges*, ICC, p. 418.

To prevent harm to his guest the old man offered his daughter and the Levite's concubine to the men (19:24). The statement reflects the enormous lengths the host went to in order to protect his guest; however, it also reflects the appallingly low status of women in ancient culture. It remained for the teachings of both the Old and New Testaments to clarify the true worth and nobility of women (Prov. 31: Rom. 16:1–2; Gal. 3:28). In a similar incident Lot offered his daughters to the men of Sodom (Gen. 19:7–8).

The old man repeated his concern that they refrain from such a disgraceful action (19:24). When the wicked men refused to listen, the Levite (the identification of "the man" is not entirely clear but seems to refer to the Levite since it was "his concubine") took his concubine and sent her outside to the men. No doubt this was out of fear for his own life and his lack of concern for his concubine the next morning would be consistent with this suggestion. The men raped and abused the concubine all night and at dawn they let her go. The concubine returned to her master's house, fell down at the door, and lay there until daylight.

It should be noted that the men of Gibeah desired a homosexual relationship with the Levite. Those guilty of such perversion are condemned to death by the Old Testament (Lev. 18:22; 20:13); the New Testament not only condemns the practice but warns that no homosexual will enter the kingdom of God (Rom. 1:24–32; 1 Cor. 6:9; Gal. 5:19–21).

D. Dismemberment of the concubine (19:27–30)

There is no indication in the text that the Levite had any concern for his concubine as he determined to leave Gibeah. In departing from the house the following morning he discovered his concubine lying in the doorway with her hands on the threshold. It appears the concubine had tried to reach the shelter of the house before she died. This account reflects not only the brutality of the men of Gibeah, but also the cold indifference of the Levite. His harsh words, "Get up; let's go," further reveal his unconcern. Then the Levite discovered that his concubine was dead; he put her body on his donkey and departed for Ephraim.

When the Levite arrived home he "cut his concubine's body into twelve pieces (19:29). The word cut (Hebrew, *natah*) is used of dividing sacrificial offerings according to their bones (Exod. 29:17; Lev. 1:6, 12; 8:20). Then the Levite sent the twelve pieces to the twelve tribes of

Israel. This act was designed to show the twelve tribes what particular sin the tribe of Benjamin was guilty of and to provoke the tribes to render judgment on the guilty tribe. A parallel summons to war took place when King Saul cut up two oxen and sent them throughout Israel to muster an army (1 Sam. 11:7). "Sending the dissected pieces of the corpse to the tribes was a symbolic act, by which the crime committed upon the murdered woman was placed before the eyes of the whole nation, to summon it to punish the crime."[7]

The statement of verse 30 should be understood as spoken by the messengers who took the parts to the twelve tribes and told the story of what the Benjamites in Gibeah had done to the concubine. Some Septuagint manuscripts reflect this, stating "And he commanded the men whom he sent out saying, Say these words to all the men of Israel, has such a thing as this ever happened from the day when the children of Israel came up out of the land of Egypt unto this day? Consider it, take counsel, and speak." The Levite was calling on the tribes to reflect on what had taken place and then seek to carry out the appropriate action because of this despicable deed.

For Further Study

1. Analyze the life of the Levite. What negative lessons can be learned from his life?

2. Is hospitality a problem today? How should a Christian show hospitality? Through use of a concordance, study the scriptural teaching concerning hospitality.

3. In a Bible dictionary or encyclopedia read articles on Gibeah, concubine, and Benjamin.

4. Cite all the features of chapter 19 that underscore the depravity of the period of Judges.

---

[7]Keil and Delitzsch, *Joshua, Judges, Ruth*, p. 446.

Chapter 11

Anarchy
(Judges 20:1–21:25)

There is a cause-effect relationship between chapters 19 and 20. When the Israelites from the other tribes heard what the Benjamites had done, they prepared for battle against them to judge the men responsible for the sin and the tribe for their refusal to release the guilty individuals.

A. Explanation of the Levite (20:1–7)

The messengers that the Levite had sent out to summon the tribes said, "Think about it! Consider it! Tell us what to do!" (19:30). The appeal yielded results, for Israelites from the northern extremity of Dan to Israel's southern town of Beersheba assembled to render judgment. Even representatives from Gilead, those living east of the Jordan, came "before the LORD in Mizpah" (20:1). This does not indicate that the sanctuary was at Mizpah at this time; rather, the tribes held a meeting in the sight of the Lord. They assembled as a judicial court in the name of the Lord.[1] The tabernacle was at Shiloh in the period of the judges (cf. Josh. 18:1; Judg. 21:19; 1 Sam. 1:3), although there were other assembly points in the nation such as Bethel, Gilgal, and Mizpah (1 Sam. 7:16).[2]

The tribes assembled as Mizpah ("watchtower"), the probable location being about eight miles north of Jerusalem at Tell en-Nasbeh. The "leaders" (literally "corners" as in 1 Kings 7:34, but here figuratively as a ruler or chief who supports or defends as in 1 Sam. 14:38; Isa. 19:13, emphasizing the stabilizing power of Israel's fighting force) met with

---

[1]Keil and Delitzsch, *Joshua, Judges, Ruth*, p. 447.
[2]See the detailed discussion in de Vaux, *Ancient Israel*, pp. 289–311.

400,000 soldiers armed with swords to carry out justice against the Benjamites. Although some reject this number of fighting men as unrealistic, the figure is not unreasonable since the men of Israel twenty years old or more numbered 601,730 prior to entering the land. The fighting force at Mizpah represented two-thirds of that number.

When the men of Israel had gathered at Mizpah, the Levite explained what had happened at Gibeah (20:4–7). The Levite indicated that the men of Gibeah intended to kill him, although that is not stated in 19:22. The Levite may have reached his conclusion on the basis of what happened to his wife; also, it may be that the Levite thrust his concubine out of the house because he feared for his own life. The Levite then reminded the fighting men that he had sent the pieces of his concubine throughout the land to notify the nation of the "lewd and disgraceful act" (20:6). The two terms are significant. "Lewd" (Hebrew, *zimma*) is frequently used of sexual perversion such as incest (Lev. 18:17; 20:14), giving a daughter into prostitution (Lev. 19:29), and adultery (Job 31:11). These sins were all punishable by death according to the Mosaic Law. "Disgraceful" (Hebrew, *nebala*), a "disregard for moral and spiritual claims,"[3] is used with reference to sexual promiscuity (Deut. 22:21; Gen. 34:7), premeditated rape (2 Sam. 13:12), adultery (Jer. 29:23), and homosexual relations (Judg. 19:23–24); see comment on 19:23. In one sense a glimmer of moral light shines here in the darkness of the times of the judges, for the men of Israel recognized that the law of Moses had been violated and they must mete out judgment.

B. Indignation of Israel (20:8–11)

The text emphasizes the unity of the tribes in judging the men of Gibeah by stating that they came as "one man" (20:8, 11). The Israelites determined to go up against Gibeah as the lot directed them. The reference to the lot is unclear. Some suggest the lot refers to setting apart one-tenth of the men to supply the provisions; others suggest it refers to determining which tribe would go up first; still others suggest it looks beyond Benjamin's defeat to the division of the Benjamite territory among the other tribes.

To facilitate this military venture the Israelites set apart one-tenth of their men to supply food provisions for the men in battle. The Hebrews were united in their endeavor (20:11; Hebrew, *haber*) of attaching

---

[3]Louis Goldberg, "כְּבָלָה," *Theological Wordbook*, vol. 2, p. 547.

pieces of material (the verb in the same word family is used; Exod. 39:4).

C. Injunction of Israel (20:12–16)

The men of Israel who had gathered against the Benjamites sent men throughout the tribe of Benjamin to admonish them for the crime and to exhort them to bring forth the guilty men for judgment of their sin. The purpose is given in 20:13: "so that we may put them to death and purge the evil from Israel." It was necessary, according to the law of Moses, to "purge" the evil from the land. The root of the word "purge" (Hebrew, *ba'ar*) means to "burn or consume"; here the word "purge" means to "*consume*, utterly remove, particularly of evil and guilt."[4]

> The most common usage of the word has to do with removing evil or evil influence from the land (20 times, 10 of which are in Deut.). If a person has committed some flagrant sin (idolatry, murder, fornication, prostitution, adultery, intranational slavery) not only must he himself be removed, but through his execution the evil which he has set in train must be removed (Deut. 13:1–5; II Sam. 4:11; I Kgs. 14:10 etc.).[5]

Deuteronomy 22:22 explicitly commands the death penalty for the sin of which the men of Gibeah were guilty in order to purge the evil from the land. The same emphasis is seen in 1 Samuel 11:12 when Saul's kingship was challenged. The purging of sin was essential to prevent disaster in the nation such as the defeat at Ai when Israel failed to judge the sin of Achan (Josh. 7).

In refusing to deliver up the guilty men, the Benjamites identified themselves with the sin and brought judgment on the entire tribe (20:13). Instead of handing over the men, the Benjamites gathered for war against their Israelite brothers. The Benjamites mobilized their forces, gathering twenty-six thousand swordsmen and seven hundred marksmen with slings. The "left-handed" (v. 16; literally, "restricted in the right hand") were skilled with the sling and the emphasis here anticipates their initial victory over the men of Israel (vv. 19–28). Left-handed warriors such as Ehud (3:15) and David's men from Ziklag (1 Chron. 12:2) were valuable in warfare. The slings that the seven hundred men used were also formidable weapons.

> The *sling*, which was employed with a left-handed motion, must not be confused with a modern schoolboy's catapult; it was a formidable weapon of war used in the Assyrian, Egyptian and Babylonian armies as well as in

---

[4]Brown, Driver, and Briggs, *Hebrew and English Lexicon*, p. 129.
[5]John N. Oswalt, "בָּעַר," *Theological Wordbook*, p. 122.

Israel. David's encounter with the Philistine, Goliath, is a telling example of the power and accuracy of this weapon (1 Sa. 17:49). It has been estimated that stones weighing up to one pound could be projected with uncanny accuracy at speeds up to 90 m.p.h.![6]

There is a seeming discrepancy in the numbers of the Benjamites in this chapter. In 20:15 their total number is 26,700 while in verses 44–47 it is recorded that 25,000 were slain and only 600 were left. Verse 35 records 25,100 were slain. The solution is not difficult. The losses mentioned in verses 44–47 are those sustained on the third day of battle; it is inconceivable that the Benjamites would have won their earlier victories (vv. 19–28) without losses. The additional 1100 Benjamites would have fallen on the first two days of battle (vv. 21, 25). Hence 1100 + 18,000 + 5000 + 2000 + 600 = 26,700. The difference between 25,100 (v. 35) and 25,000 (vv. 44–46) is seen in that only the full thousands are mentioned in the latter verses.[7]

D. Preparation for battle (20:17–18)

There was clearly a disparity in the alignment of the sides: 26,700 Benjamites versus 400,000 men of Israel. Prior to the battle the Israelites went up to Bethel to inquire of the Lord concerning who would be the first to venture into battle against the Benjamites. Although the tabernacle was still at Shiloh (Josh. 18:1; Judg. 21:19; 1 Sam. 1:3), the ark was at times transported into battle (cf. 1 Sam. 4:3). To avoid the trek northward to Shiloh, the ark was brought down to Bethel, only five miles north of Mizpah. In response to their query the Lord instructed them to send Judah into battle first.

E. Expedition Against Benjamin (20:19–48)

1. *First encounter* (20:19–23)

Judah may have been chosen because their territory was next to Benjamin and they would have been familiar with the terrain. The men of Judah proceeded in battle formation against the Benjamites and in the encounter twenty-two thousand Israelites were slain. As a result the Israelites went up to the ark of the Lord and wept (20:23). When they inquired of the Lord, He again sent them into battle and they took up their battle positions once more (v. 22).

---

[6]Cundall and Morris, *Judges and Ruth*, p. 201.
[7]Keil and Delitzsch, *Joshua, Judges, Ruth*, pp. 450–51.

2. *Second encounter* (20:24–28)

On the second day of battle (not necessarily sequential days), the Benjamites inflicted further losses on the Israelites as eighteen thousand men of Israel fell in battle. The contrite attitude of the Israelites is noteworthy. They went up to Bethel where they wept, fasted, and offered burnt offerings and fellowship offerings. Both were voluntary offerings and the burnt offering was a consecratory offering that signified complete surrender to God (cf. Lev. 1:1–17), while the fellowship offering signified communion with the Lord (cf. Lev. 3:1–17).[8] Repentance was foundational to these offerings, and Israel now turned to the Lord in genuine humility and repentance.

While the reason for Israel's two defeats is not explicitly stated, it may be inferred by their attitude.

> The congregation now discovered, from this repeated defeat, that the Lord had withdrawn His grace, and was punishing them. (Their sin was) their strong self-consciousness, and great confidence in their own might and power. They had indeed inquired of God (Elohim) who should open the conflict; but they had neglected to humble themselves before Jehovah the covenant God, in the consciousness not only of their own weakness and sinfulness, but also of grief at the moral corruption of their brother-tribe.[9]

Once more the Israelites inquired of the Lord whether they were to go to war against the Benjamites, presumably with a humble attitude in contrast to their previous requests (20:27). The text indicates the ark of the Lord was temporarily at Bethel, a worship shrine, although the tabernacle remained at Shiloh.

The mention of Phinehas, a son of Eleazar and grandson of Aaron, indicates that this narrative reflects events early in the time of the judges. That the Lord had received the offerings of the Israelites is indicated by the fact that He promised them victory on the following day.

3. *Third encounter* (20:29–48)

a) *Invasion of Israel* (20:29–36)

Since Israel had been repulsed by two direct attacks on Gibeah, they decided on a change in strategy. Setting an ambush similar to Joshua's strategy for the conquest of Ai (Josh. 8:4–29), a main force of Israelites advanced on Gibeah and lured the Benjamites out of the city while a

---

[8] A. F. Rainey, "Sacrifice and Offerings," ZPEB, 5:205–8.
[9] Keil and Delitzsch, *Joshua, Judges, Ruth*, p. 452.

contingent lay in wait behind the city. The Israelites purposely re-
treated as the Benjamites attacked, causing the attackers to leave their
city behind in their pursuit of the fleeing Israelites. This strategy
caused the Benjamites to think they were again victorious as they killed
thirty men in the open field and on the roads leading north to Bethel
and Gibeah. Since the text literally reads "Gibeah in the field," it may
suggest one fork of the divided road led down into the field from the
town of Gibeah.

Both the deception and the strategy are seen in verse 32. The deceived Benjamites thought this battle would follow the same pattern as
the previous two battles, but for the men of Israel the battle was
following their premeditated plan; they were successful in drawing the
men of Gibeah out of the city. Then the men of Israel took their places
at Baal Tamar (a site unknown today) in preparation for an assault on
the Benjamites. Meanwhile, ten thousand men west of Gibeah came
out of hiding and advanced toward Gibeah. The reference to "west of
Gibeah" (v. 33; Maareh-geba, NASB), meaning "meadow of Gibeah (or
Geba)," is not clear but may be connected with the open field west of
Gibeah. While such a field would not have concealed the ambush party
the explanation may be that the ten thousand men advanced on Gibeah
across the meadow after coming out of their hiding place.

When the ten thousand men advanced toward the Benjamites, they
prevented a retreat to the city. The men of Gibeah were not caught
between two armies of Israel; only at this point did they realize they
had been tricked and their defeat was certain. The ultimate source of
the victory was the Lord, who enabled Israel to strike down 25,100
Benjamites on that day. Thus the Benjamites were judged for the sin of
Gibeah.[10]

b) *Destruction of Gibeah* (20:37–48)

The general explanation of the battle is given in 20:29–36 and the
specific details are given in verses 37–48. When the men of Gibeah
had been lured out into the open, the ambush party quickly invaded
the city. Entrance would have been relatively simple since the fighting
men had departed. The Israelites slew the inhabitants and set the city
ablaze, sending up a great cloud of smoke (v. 38). The smoke was a
prearranged signal for the main Israelite army. Having feigned defeat,

---

[10]For two differing diagrams illustrating the movement of the battle see Cundall and
Morris, *Judges and Ruth*, p. 205, and Aharoni and Avi-Yonah, *The Macmillan Bible
Atlas*, p. 56.

they now turned and pursued the men of Gibeah. The "column" (Hebrew, 'ammud) of smoke (v. 40) is interesting to note, for the Hebrew term for "column" is also used with reference to the Lord leading Israel by the "pillar" of cloud by day and the "pillar" of fire at night (Exod. 13:21–22; 14:24).

When the Benjamites saw that disaster threatened them, they fled toward the desert (20:42). "The wilderness lay to the east of Gibeah, the steep uncultivated hill-sides and ravines in which the Highlands of Ephraim break down to the Jordan valley."[11] The Benjamites hoped to escape in this rugged area, but the Israelites pursued them and killed 18,000 Benjamites. The surviving Benjamites fled toward the rock of Rimmon, but five thousand were cut down along the road, while two thousand more were struck down as the Israelites pursued them as far as Gidom (v. 45). The rock of Rimmon provided a natural protection for the fugitives, for ravines were on the north, south, and west sides and there were numerous caves in which the Benjamites could hide. Only six hundred Benjamites remained alive, and these hid at Rimmon four months.

Since the tribe of Benjamin had failed to deliver the wicked men to the Israelites for judgment, the entire tribe of Benjamin experienced judgment as the men of Israel now devastated the tribe's territory by killing the inhabitants and cattle and then setting the cities on fire. In so doing the Israelites carried out the demands of the Mosaic Law (Deut. 13:12–18).

F. Preservation of the tribe of Benjamin (21:1–24)

1. *Sorrow of Israel* (21:1–7)

When the battle with the Benjamites was over, two major problems became evident: (1) In their determination to avenge the sin of the men of Gibeah, the men of Israel had almost exterminated an entire tribe; only six hundred Benjamites remained. The extensive killing may have been revenge for the two earlier losses as much as it was judgment for the sin of Gibeah. (2) The Israelites had sworn at Mizpah that none of them would give their daughters in marriage to a Benjamite (21:1). This occurred at the time when the tribes had gathered at Mizpah for battle against the Benjamites (20:1). The problem now became apparent: how would they find Hebrew wives for the remain-

---

[11]Moore, *A Critical and Exegetical Commentary on Judges*, p. 440.

ing six hundred Benjamite men to avoid their complete extermination?

The people went up to Bethel where the ark of the Lord was and wept and lamented over the dilemma. The lamentation "involved the wish that God might show them the way to avert the threatened destruction of the missing tribe, and build up the six hundred who remained."[12] They revealed their sincerity by offering burnt offerings and fellowship offerings.

It is unclear why the Israelites built an altar at Bethel to offer sacrifices when an altar already existed there (21:4; cf. 20:26). Some suggest the altar mentioned in 21:4 was constructed at Mizpah; the text, however, seems to indicate it was at Bethel. A better suggestion is that this was an additional altar since the existing altar was not large enough when all the tribes offered sacrifices commemorating their victory.[13]

In order to solve the problem of providing wives for the six hundred Benjamites, the Israelites sought to discover who among the tribes had not responded to the call assembling all the tribes in judgment. On determining who had been absent, they would carry out the solemn oath; namely, to impose the death penalty on those who had failed to respond.

> The definite article may visualize the most solemn adjuration involving the death penalty familiar in the Twelve Adjurations in the sacrament of the Covenant (Dt. 27:15–26) and apodictic laws in the Book of the Covenant (e.g. Exod. 21:12, 15, 16, 17; 22:19–20), which use the formula "he shall surely be put to death."[14]

By effecting this solemn oath they would inflict the death penalty on those who had ignored the summons and thereby obtain virgin women for the Benjamite men.

2. *Slaughter of Jabesh Gilead* (21:8–12)

When the Israelites inquired who had been absent, it was stated that no one from Jabesh Gilead had participated in the judgment of Benjamin. To prevent a fatal error, the Israelites counted the people and found that no one from Jabesh Gilead was present. Jabesh Gilead (its name is preserved in the Wadi Yabis) was located nine miles southeast of Beth Shan. From this town four hundred Benjamite men would receive their wives. This was a most important connection since the

---

[12]Keil and Delitzsch, *Joshua, Judges, Ruth*, pp. 458–59.
[13]Fausset, *Critical and Expository Commentary*, p. 329.
[14]Gray, *Joshua, Judges and Ruth*, CB, p. 391.

inhabitants of Jabesh Gilead were descendants of Manasseh, whose grandmother was Rachel. Rachel was also the mother of Benjamin (Gen. 35:18); hence the people of Jabesh Gilead and Benjamin had common blood bonds.

As a result of their discovery the Israelites sent twelve thousand fighting men to Jabesh Gilead to put all the men, married women, and children to death (21:10–11). The command to "kill" (v. 11; "utterly destroy," NASB) is important to the discussion. The underlying Hebrew word, *herem*, is equivalent to the Greek word *anathema*, and is used of "devoting to destruction cities of Canaanites and other neighbours of Isr., *exterminating* inhabitants, and destroying or appropriating their possessions."[15] *Herem* is frequently found with reference to God's judgment of the depraved Canaanites (cf. Josh. 6:17, 21).

> Usually *haram* means a ban for utter destruction, the compulsory dedication of something which impedes or resists God's work, which is considered to be accursed before God. The idea first appears in Num. 21:2–3, where the Israelites vowed that, if God would enable them to defeat a southern Canaanite king, they would "utterly destroy" (i.e. consider as devoted and accordingly utterly destroy) his cities. This word it used regarding almost all the cities which Joshua's troops destroyed (e.g. Jericho, Josh 6:21; Ai, Josh 8:26; Makkedah, Josh 10:28; Hazor, Josh 11:11), thus indicating the rationale for their destruction. In Deut. 7:2–6, the command for this manner of destruction is given, with the explanation following that, otherwise, these cities would lure the Israelites away from the Lord (cf. Deut. 20:17–18). Any Israelite city that harbored idolators was to be "utterly destroyed" (Deut. 13:12–15; cf. Ex. 22:19).[16]

Because the people of Jabesh Gilead had refused to respond to the summons, they placed themselves under the curse and judgment.

The Israelites carried out their plan and destroyed the inhabitants of the city, but they spared four hundred virgin women whom they brought to the camp at Shiloh where the tabernacle was located.

3. *Selection of wives* (21:13–15)

The Israelites now convinced the six hundred Benjamites who still remained in hiding at the rock of Rimmon, of their peaceful intentions. Having come out of hiding, the Benjamites were given the virgins from Jabesh Gilead as their wives. Yet there were not enough women for the six hundred men—two hundred still had no wives. The statement of

---

[15]Brown, Driver, and Briggs, *Hebrew and English Lexicon*, p. 355.
[16]Leon J. Wood, "חָרַם," *Theological Wordbook*, vol. 1, p. 324.

verse 14b anticipates what was to take place in 21:19–24. The sorrow of the Israelites in verse 15 further emphasizes that they wanted to help the Benjamites find wives; however, their vow prevented them from giving the Benjamites their own daughters.

4. *Situation for the remaining Benjamites* (21:16–18)

The elders now similarly expressed their concern over the two hundred Benjamites who had no wives. In the literal Hebrew the exclamation of the elders in verse 17 is elliptical, affirming, "An inheritance for the escaped of Benjamin," meaning that the Benjamites needed to have heirs. The term "inheritance" (Hebrew, *yerushsha*) normally refers to land and the term indicates land (cf. Josh. 1:15; 12:6–7). The emphasis here, no doubt, is that Benjamin should have a posterity that would continue to possess the land that had been allotted to them. Nonetheless, the Israelites were prohibited from giving the Benjamites wives from their own tribes because of their oath (21:18).

5. *Selection of additional wives* (21:19–24)

The problem would ultimately be solved at the annual feast at Shiloh. The law prescribed three annual pilgrimage feasts (Exod. 34:23)—Passover, Pentecost, and Tabernacles. It is not clear which feast took place on this occasion. The dancing may indicate the Feast of Passover, patterned after the dancing by Miriam and the women following the Red Sea crossing (Exod. 15:20). The rejoicing in the vineyards, however, would suggest the joyous celebration at the grape harvest (cf. 9:27), which would indicate this was the Feast of Tabernacles.

The elders of Israel instructed the two hundred remaining Benjamites as to how they were to obtain wives for themselves (21:19ff.). As the Israelite women would join in the "dancing" (21:21; Hebrew, *mecholah*), each Benjamite was to rush out of the vineyards, seize one of the women, and flee to the territory of Benjamin. Dancing was not unusual in Hebrew worship (Ps. 149:3). David danced as the ark was brought to Jerusalem (2 Sam. 6:14–15); dancing occurred in commemoration of a victory (Exod. 15:20) and took place at festivals (Judg. 21:19). The dance was performed by turning and skipping, with the dancers wreathed with sweet-smelling flowers or carrying ivy-wreathed wands, beautiful branches, and palm fronds. Ultimately, the joyous dancing anticipated the consummation of the age when the Lord would turn mourning into dancing (Ps. 30:11).[17]

If the fathers or brothers of the brides would complain, the elders of Israel promised to support the Benjamite action. The elders would encourage the fathers to let the Benjamites have their daughters since the Benjamites had not received wives for themselves in battle. The elders would further explain that the Israelites would not be violating the oath since technically they had not given their daughters to the Benjamites (21:22).

The suggestion must have pleased the Benjamites since they secured wives for themselves and returned to their own territory and rebuilt their cities. As a result all six hundred of the remaining Benjamite men had wives whereby they could continue to exist as a tribe.

G. Conclusion to the Book of Judges (21:25)

The reader is reminded of the theme of the Book of Judges as the narrative draws to a conclusion: "In those days Israel had no king; everyone did as he saw fit." The concluding statement explains the many unusual happenings in Judges—the idolatry, the immorality, and the anarchy. There was no adequate mediator to unite the people of God; everyone did as he saw fit.

For Further Study

1. Through a concordance study of the word tabernacle trace the movement of the tabernacle before its final location at Jerusalem.

2. Examine the action of the Israelites toward the Benjamites. Was their action justified?

3. Analyze the major factors that resulted in the apostasy during the period of the judges.

4. List the positive and negative lessons you have learned from the Book of Judges. What are the positive paths to pursue? What are the negative factors to avoid?

---

[17]H. Eising, "חול," *Theological Dictionary*, pp. 260–64.

BIBLIOGRAPHY

Aharoni, Yohanan. *The Land of the Bible*. Philadelphia: Westminster Press, 1967.

Aharoni, Yohanan and Avi-Yonah, Michael. *The Macmillan Bible Atlas*. New York: Macmillan, 1968.

Albright, William Foxwell. *From the Stone Age to Christianity*. Garden City, N.Y.: Doubleday, 1957.

_____ . *Archaeology and the Religion of Israel*, 3rd ed. Baltimore: Johns Hopkins Press, 1953.

Baly, Denis. *The Geography of the Bible*. New York: Harper & Row, 1974.

Boling, Robert G. *Judges* in *The Anchor Bible* Garden City, N.Y.: Doubleday & Company, 1975.

Botterweck, G. Johannes and Ringgren, Helmer. *Theological Dictionary of the Old Testament*, vols. 1–4. Trans. John T. Willis, Geoffrey W. Bromiley, and David E. Green. Grand Rapids: Eerdmans, 1974–1980.

Bright, John. *A History of Israel*, 2nd ed. Philadelphia: Westminster Press, 1962.

Brown, Francis, Driver, S. R., and Briggs, Charles A. *A Hebrew and English Lexicon of the Old Testament*. Oxford: At the Clarendon Press, 1968.

Bruce, F. F. "Judges," *New Bible Commentary: Revised*. Grand Rapids: Eerdmans, 1970.

Bullinger, E. W. *Figures of Speech Used in the Bible*. Grand Rapids: Baker, 1968.

Cassel, Paulus. "The Book of Judges," *Lange's Commentary on the Holy Scriptures*, vol. 2. Grand Rapids: Zondervan, 1960 reprint.

Cooke, G. A. *The Book of Judges* in *The Cambridge Bible for Schools and Colleges*. Cambridge: At the University Press, 1913.

de Vaux, Roland. *Ancient Israel*, 2 vols. New York: McGraw-Hill, 1965.

Fausset, A. R. *A Critical and Expository Commentary on the Book of Judges*. Minneapolis: James & Klock Publishing Co., 1977 reprint.

Finegan, Jack. *Light from the Ancient Past*, 2 vols. Princeton: Princeton University Press, 1959.

Garstang, John. *Joshua-Judges*. Grand Rapids: Kregel, 1978.

Girdlestone, Robert A. *Synonyms of the Old Testament* (Grand Rapids: Eerdmans, 1974 reprint).

Gray, John. *Joshua, Judges and Ruth* in *The Century Bible*. Greenwood, S.C.: The Attic Press, 1967.

Harris, R. Laird, Archer, Gleason L., Jr., and Waltke, Bruce K., eds. *Theological Wordbook of the Old Testament*, 2 vols. Chicago: Moody, 1980.

Harrison, R. K. *Old Testament Times*, Grand Rapids: Eerdmans, 1970.

_____. *Introduction to the Old Testament* (Grand Rapids: Eerdmans, 1969).

Jamieson, Robert, Fausset, A. R., and Brown, David. *A Commentary Critical, Experimental, and Practical on the Old and New Testaments*, 6 vols. Grand Rapids: Eerdmans, 1945 reprint.

Keil, C. F., and Delitzsch, F. *Joshua, Judges, Ruth* in *Biblical Commentary on the Old Testament*. Grand Rapids: Eerdmans, 1968 reprint.

Moore, George Foot. *A Critical and Exegetical Commentary on Judges* in *The International Critical Commentary*. New York: Charles Scribner's Sons, 1906.

Payne, J. Barton. *The Theology of the Older Testament*. Grand Rapids: Zondervan, 1962.

Pfeiffer, Charles F., ed. *The Biblical World*. Grand Rapids: Baker, 1966.

————. "Judges," *The Wycliffe Bible Commentary*. Chicago: Moody, 1962.

Pfeiffer, Charles F., and Vos, Howard F. *The Wycliffe Historical Geography of Bible Lands*. Chicago: Moody, 1967.

Tenney, Merrill C.. gen. ed. *The Zondervan Pictorial Encyclopedia of the Bible*, 5 vols. Grand Rapids: Zondervan, 1975.

Thompson, J. A. *The Bible Archaeology*, Grand Rapids: Eerdmans, 1962.

Unger, Merrill F. *Archaeology and the Old Testament*. Grand Rapids: Zondervan, 1954.

Unger, Merrill F., and White, William Jr. eds. *Nelson's Expository Dictionary of the Old Testament*. Nashville: Thomas Nelson Publishers, 1980.

Wood, Leon. *Distressing Days of the Judges*. Grand Rapids: Zondervan, 1975.